Royal Copley
(plus Royal Windsor and Spaulding)

By
Leslie C. Wolfe and Marjorie A. Wolfe

COLLECTOR BOOKS
A Division of Schroeder Publishing Co., Inc.

Please address all correspondence to:
Joseph M. Devine
1411 3rd Street
Council Bluffs, Iowa 51503-6805
Telephone: (712) 328-7305

Additional copies of this book may be ordered from:

Collector Books
P.O. Box 3009
Paducah, Kentucky 42002-3009

@$14.95. Add $2.00 for postage and handling.

Printed by IMAGE GRAPHICS, INC., Paducah, Kentucky

Dedication

This book is graciously dedicated to
Marjorie A. Wolfe
In loving memory of her husband
Leslie C. Wolfe
1918–1987

Without their dedication and determination the story of the Spaulding China Company would never have been told. They have earned and deserve the credit for this story.

Joseph M. Devine

Table of Contents

Dedication 3

Foreword..6

Acknowledgements and Appreciation 7

The Story of the Spaulding China Company 9

A Broad View of Royal Copley..................................15

How to Identify Royal Copley 19

Photos and Script:

    a. Royal Copley..................................22

    b. Royal Windsor 98

    c. Spaulding..................................102

Solving the Puzzle..................................107

Some of Spaulding's Special People:

    a. Morris Feinberg..................................110

    b. James G. Eardley..................................113

    c. Anthony Priolo..................................115

    d. Margaret Kadisch 117

Bibliography and Source Material 126

Price Guide 127

Foreword

As time goes on, the name SPAULDING will become one of the "jewels" in the crown of Sebring. Long a center for the production of pottery and china, Sebring, Ohio, bears a name synonymous with that of Zanesville, Roseville, and Crooksville.

The Spaulding China Company was organized in 1941 with actual production beginning in 1942. Of the many persons associated with Spaulding, the name MORRIS FEINBERG stands out alone. From 1941 to 1957 and during the time of liquidation, he was both the **president** and **guiding spirit** of the Spaulding operation.

Spaulding's success can be attributed to their motto **"Gift Shop Merchandise at Chain Store Prices"**. It was Spaulding that revolutionized the era of chain store taste for ceramics.

This book will deal mainly with Royal Copley with some emphasis on Royal Windsor and items marked Spaulding. Approximately 85% of everything made at Spaulding was Royal Copley.

Without a doubt most of the items produced at Spaulding will soon become collector items and prized by the many collectors across the country. It is the purpose and intent of this book to reveal the beauty, color, style, and design of all that belonged to Spaulding.

It is also our desire to provide a book that will be helpful for both collectors and dealers. We are taking the liberty of showing items made in as many colors as possible. This will be very helpful in ordering and buying.

A suggested value for pricing will be included for every item pictured in the book. We are disregarding prices that are not realistic. We do feel that in pricing there should be room for future growth. Please remember that pricing is only a guide and should not be considered as Holy Writ.

Acknowledgments and Appreciation

There is no way to adequately thank people who have given so generously of their time and effort in our behalf. The following people are more deserving than any words or thanks we can offer. It was their help, encouragement, and personal interest that made this book possible. If the book has any merit the credit rightfully belongs to them.

Alabama - James Ellett.

California - Anthony and Joan Priolo.

Florida - Joe Feinberg, Morris Feinberg.

Illinois - Ed Ashley, Gladys Collier, Louie Ella Davis, Carol De Moss, Gene Ellison, Ruby Gano, Dr. George Godfrey, Wm. Goff, Jan Granse, Judy Hudson, Dr. Lawrence B. Hunt, Inez Jenkins, Virginia and Lawrence Keefe, Hildegard Lary, Ed Lohr, Dee Long, Charles Lumsdon, Dorothy Moody, Chris Morrow, Dr. Iain Paul, and David and Nancy Peterson.

Indiana - Elizabeth and Chas. Boyce, Ted Haun, and Sharon and Bob Huxford.

Iowa - Laura Erickson and Warren and Barb White.

Kentucky - Dana Curtis.

Michigan - Don Brewer, Daria Killinger, Norma Killinger, Nora Koch, Betty Newbound, Dr. Richard W. Pippen, and Rick Summerlee.

Mississippi - Betty Bell.

New York - Ed Gisel.

Ohio - Betty and Floyd Carson, Lindley Carson, Shirley Charney, Delores Drown, Charlotte H. Eardley, Mrs. James G. Eardley, Shirley Graff, Margaret Kadisch, Paul Nowack, and Lillian Szafranski.

Oregon - Ron Perrick

Texas - Rena London

Every author is indebted to those wonderful people who are willing to share and loan items from their collection. Only through the generosity of these people were we able to show so many lovely and hard-to-find items. Some of these people drove over 1,000 miles to bring items for us to see and use for the book. We are proud to list their names: James Ellett, Carol De Moss, Judy Hudson, Daria Killinger, Norma Killinger, Ed Lohr, Betty Newbound, David and Nancy Peterson, Rick Summerlee, and Barb and Warren White.

The Story of the Spaulding China Company

It seems strange that a company as outstanding as Spaulding China should remain for all practical purposes unknown and unheard of in all the material that has been written on Ohio Pottery. Even the renowned author, Lois Lehner, mentions in one of her articles in the *Depression Glass Daze* that at one time she stood in the building where Royal Copley was made and didn't know it. Usually when someone attempts to write a book on a certain subject there is literature available from which to glean certain facts and information. We were forced to tell the story of Spaulding the hard way, to begin with nothing, and finally piece the story together bit by bit. It has been an interesting challenge and from this adventure we hope to reveal the "glory" that was Spaulding's. The story of Spaulding is unique in many ways as we shall endeavor to tell.

It all began at Sebring, Ohio, an area long noted for pottery and fine ceramic ware. Although Spaulding was born at Sebring it was, we might say, the "child" of Morris Feinberg. Without his guidance, foresight, and creative genius there would have been no Spaulding China Company. Here was a man who, singularly, would have been successful in any endeavor he might have chosen.

Contrary to dates and figures found elsewhere Spaulding did not begin operation until 1942. It was during the first six months of 1942 that production actually began. From a brief history of Sebring, Ohio, published in 1949 in connection with Sebring's 50th Anniversary a few interesting facts are noted. The company began operation in a garage on East Ohio Avenue. Needing more room the plant moved temporarily to the abandoned plant of the Alliance Vitreous China Company. Finally through the efforts of the Sebring Business Men they acquired the location of the old Sebring Rubber Company. The company installed the finest and most up-to-date machinery they could find at the time. They started with a straight tunnel kiln and a decorating kiln that fired at a lower temperature for decal and gold decorating. Due to increased demand and production, the straight tunnel kiln and decorating kiln were dismantled around 1947 or possibly 1948. With the installation of a large continuous circular kiln, they were able to operate 24 hours a day and in 10 hour cycles. They were in operation every day of the year except for a two week period. With the installation of the large continuous circular kiln, it was possible to fire about 1,500 dozen or 18,000 items per day. And happy to say, with this kiln, only one firing was required.

Most persons seem to believe that Sebring became a center for china and ceramic ware because of its clay. This was not the case. It was the supply of coal and water that made Sebring the center it has been for so many years. The clay for the Spaulding China Company was shipped in from other states such as Georgia and Florida with a much needed No. 5 ball clay coming from England.

The officers of the Spaulding China Company were: Morris Feinberg, president, Mount Vernon, New York; Irving Miller, vice president, Jamaica, Long Island, New York; Daniel Eisenberg, vice president and assistant secretary, Plainfield, New Jersey; and David Borowitz, secretary, of Chicago, Illinois. The main office was located in the Empire State Building, New York City, New York.

The plant was operated by the following personnel: James G. Eardley, general manager; E.F. Cannell, production control; James Simpson, production; Albert Sines, maintenance supervisor; Clyde Hardy, decorating and design; Frank Weizenecker, quality control and shipping; Barbara Berry, office manager; Joan Haberland, billing; Margaret Kadisch, art and design; Carmen Lewis, design; and Dennie Welch, dipping.

Pearl Harbor and World War II meant the end of many ceramic items received from Japan and other places outside the United States. Because ceramics were not strategic to the war effort, all companies producing ceramics ware were given the signal to increase their production.

It seems that everything Spaulding did was carefully considered, planned, and worked out. The name for the company was given very special consideration. The name **Spaulding** rather than **Spalding** was selected as the name for the company. It was the **u** in the way the word was spelled that made the difference. The word **Spaulding** has an English air about it and carries with it a note of sophistication. And what about the words **Royal Copley**, and **Royal Windsor**? They were carefully considered, also, and not "pulled out of the air" so to speak. For most people, the names "Royal Copley" and "Royal Windsor" suggest an association or connotation with royalty or something very fine. And the clever use of terms continue: Regal Assortment, Lennox Assortment, Carlton Assortment, Crown Assortment, Essex Assortment, and Oxford Assortment. These assortments were merely a grouping of certain birds, wall pockets, vases, and figurines into cartons of various kinds. They were sold this way and it was an efficient and convenient way of processing the orders. None of the cartons or assortments were opened. Thus, the assortment principle was a bit of merchandising that proved to be popular as well as profitable for the company.

The Spaulding operation was unique in many ways and this contributed greatly to the volume of sales and the popularity of the products. First of all, the operation was one that stressed the importance of **design** and **quality**. Spaulding soon learned that it didn't cost anymore to make items of fine quality and design than it did "junk". So their motto became **"Gift Shop Merchandise at Chain Store Prices"**. It was this emphasis on design and quality that changed the taste of chain stores for ceramic ware. In fact we can say it was Spaulding that revolutionized the era of chain store taste for ceramics. And it wasn't long until competitors learned the lesson from Spaulding. Secondly, Spaulding maintained one of the cleanest and most immaculate plants of any around. All items were shipped in strawless and standard cartons that held up well and prevented damage and breakage. However, during the height of the war when the shortage of cartons was critical, many items were shipped in cartons from stores and places of business of various kinds. It wasn't unusual for many orders to be packed in cartons bearing the term "Kosher" on the outside. Thirdly, the plant was one of the most smoothly run in the country and won safety awards time and time again. The working relationship among the workers was one of which few companies could boast. The whole operation was without a doubt one of the finest and most efficient in the nation. Of all that we might say about personnel, the name David Eardley is one of the most significant in the whole history of the Spaulding operation. He stands among the giants of the company. Here was a man trusted completely by both his boss and his fellow workers. Morris Feinberg, the president, had the ability to select people of special talent to implement his desires, goals, and wishes. He had such confidence in David Eardley that Mr. Eardley was permitted to sign checks personally for over a million dollars at a time. That was a **lot** of money at that time! Very seldom does a man like that come along. Fourthly, Spaulding experienced no inventory difficulties and at all times knew exactly where they were. Due to strict inventory keeping, they were able to change production every two weeks. This was an innovation few companies were able to duplicate. It was all a part of the novel and efficient operation at Spaulding.

Mould making was a big operation at Spaulding. Altogether Spaulding had 50 casters (all men) and each one worked with 50 to 100 moulds depending on size and the number of cavities. Thus, there were times when as many as 4,000 moulds were in operation at one time. The mould department was kept busy not only making moulds for new items but replacing those in current production. After about 100 fillings most moulds were "worn out" and destroyed.

Another big department at Spaulding was the Decorating Department. There was a total of 35 decorators (all women) and it was from this department that the rich, blending colors were selected and applied.

Lamps were made at Spaulding. However, only lamp bases were made. Most of the lamps made at Spaulding were made early and were similar to the little bud vases and pitchers that started Spaulding on its way. Most of the lamps were made in various styles with floral decals. For the most part these lamp bases were made for only a few customers, the most important one being the Bradley Manufacturing Company of Chicago, of which David Borowitz, a stockholder in the Spaulding China Company, was president. Being sold and produced in this manner, paper labels as a rule were not applied. However, we have found a few of these same decal lamps bearing a lovely Spaulding paper label.

So many of the items marked "Royal Windsor" and "Spaulding" were made for the florist trade. The "Planters of the Month" or "Books for Remembrance" series are good examples. All items produced at the Spaulding plant were geared to demand, popularity, and the number of orders coming in. Royal Windsor for the most part was made later and represented only modest production. Copley was so popular and such a big item it tended to overshadow everything else that was made.

Although the quality of Royal Windsor and items marked "Spaulding" were not superior to Royal Copley, the items commanded a higher price just because they were handled by department stores.

How easy the story of Spaudling China Company would have been had all items been stamped or marked with raised letters. Fortunately many items were marked, but so many left the plant with only a sticker or paper label. And over the years the labels were removed or washed off. How thankful we are that so many Copley items, Royal Windsor, and Spaulding items bear their original labels. We are conscious of the fact we are working in virgin territory and it "just may be" we have failed to include some items that should have been included and included some items that should not have been included. We are hoping the book will become so popular that within a matter of time we can update everything and resolve any mistakes we have made.

We are relying upon all the evidence we have gained here and there. Familiarity and study is of great help in identification and comments from collectors of long standing have been invaluable.

Without a doubt every item produced at the Spaulding plant was given a paper label. However, there is a lot of confusion concerning the paper labels. It is interesting to note that some Royal Copley items can be found with a Spaulding label and some Royal Windsor items can be found with a Royal Copley label. For the most part we have been able to identify an item by characteristics other than that of a label. With so many items being produced it is easy to see how paper labels might have ended up on the wrong item. Really, it doesn't make any difference as it all came from the same plant. However, for the most part, the right "sticker" did get "stuck" to the right item. Again, we want to stress the fact that it was Royal Copley that was sold almost exclusively to the chain stores. Good merchandising has many fine points and there are reasons why many things are done. A name can make a lot of difference in sales. It certainly did at Spaulding. If the real truth were known it "just" may be that certain items sold better if a certain label were applied. The authors have taken a lot of liberty here but after all it is conceivable that the idea of "giving them what they want" is nothing more than good business.

The company prospered, growing in volume to become at its peak the second largest art-ware pottery in the United States.

With the end of World War II the tastes and attitudes of people began to change. About a year before the factory closed, the company, in order to meet competition and changing demands, began to produce items combined or associated with wire goods. This was the "thing" at that time.

It was during this time that most companies began to experience labor difficulties of various kinds and Spaulding was no exception. During this time of change and adjustment there was, everywhere, a deterioration of morals in business. Many stores began to cancel orders without any intention of fulfilling their part of the contract. In fact many businesses abused their supplier.

Without a doubt it was severe competition from the Japanese that hastened the decision to cease operation at Spaulding, for the Japanese were flooding the market with decorative pottery at very competitive prices. And to make it worse, wage rates in Sebring were the highest in the pottery industry in the United States.

With the approach of the sixties it was obvious the nation had entered an age and time in which the good, old established ways of doing business were gone. Morris Feinberg was a man who loved business and work; but when it reached the point of interfering with his peace of mind, he considered it time to get out of the **rat race**. Therefore, in 1957 he retired but before doing so honored the orders and contracts of customers by turning them over to a near-by company, China Craft, to fill. For a period of almost two years such orders and contracts were filled. It was a rather natural kind of business arrangment as Mr. R.H. Brown, the president of China Craft, was formerly with Spaulding. Mr. R.H. Brown was not the first to leave Spaulding to form his own company.

George Stanford, a former manager at Spaulding, left Spaulding and formed the Stanford Pottery Company. It was Stanford that made the lovely Corn Pattern that is becoming popular among collectors.

Before we close the story of Spaulding, we would like to add that Irving Miller deserves a special place in the history of the Spaulding China Company. He was an early partner of Morris Feinberg. In those early days while Morris was making frequent trips between New York and Sebring, it was Irving Miller who headed up the sales. Irving Miller, vice president, not only headed up sales but approved many of the items that were to go into production. He was, in our estimation, another giant in the story of Spaulding.

Spaulding was first sold to a Mr. Shiffman who was in the plumbing business. He made primarily small sinks for mobile homes but the operation was not successful. His problem was solved through the help and guidance of Morris Feinberg. There was no foreclosure but through a financial arrangement Mr. Shiffman was relieved of his obligation.

Vacant for a few years, the plant was sold in 1964 to Mr. Eugene T. Meskill, president of Holiday Designs, Inc. They made primarily canisters, cookie jars, teapots, and accessory items.

In May of 1982 the plant was sold once more to Mr. Richard C. Durstein of Pittsburgh, Pennsylvania. Mr. Meskill remained with the company for an indefinite period of time. Thus, the story of this special plant ends here. But the GLORY of Spaulding will ever speak to us!

A Broad View of Royal Copley

Royal Copley--America's latest collectible! Already, before anything has been written on the subject, the supply is rapidly disappearing from flea markets, garage sales, and those stores handling the later collectibles.

Copley entered the scene as a collectible for several reasons:

a. Its rich, blending colors and quality of design quickly caught the eye of collectors.

b. It provided a new outlet for collectors who had reached the limit with many other collectibles.

c. Prices for the most part are modest and within the reach of everyone.

d. Copley can be found with ease although many pieces remain to be recognized.

e. Most Royal Copley items, by virtue of their style and character, have a strong personal appeal. So many of the items are associated with beautiful flowers, colorful birds, and those animals that appeal to our human emotions.

Copley was bound to catch on as some of the designers were the best in the business. They gave common production ware a sophistication afforded many of our finer wares. However, it must be pointed out that Royal Copley, although very colorful and beautifully designed, lacks the ceramic quality and individual treatment afforded the truly fine pieces. This ware was mass produced for a ready market with little or no personal treatment. Although air brushed almost exclusively, the overall results were unusually lovely and appealing.

What a pity no records were kept of the various items produced. And Spaulding had no "morgue" where examples of the various items produced were kept and stored. No one ever dreamed that the bulk of the production lines of the Spaulding China Company would, within a matter of a few years, become prized collector items. Had it not been for the merchandising genius of Morris Feinberg, the name Royal Copley would be primarily a term unknown to anyone. Copley had an appeal that "reached out and touched."

So much variety exists in Royal Copley that a collector can select any area he or she desires. There are figurines of all kinds, planters of all descriptions, vases of every design, wall planters of unbelievable quantity, and various combinations of planters and pockets made either to hang on the wall or rest on a table.

Collectors will find many colors from which to choose and some items may be found in as many as 4, 5, or more colors. There seems to be no limit on the number of items that are showing up. Some were made for only a short time and some were produced in very large quantities. The items produced for only a short time are the premium items of today. The practice of producing many items in pairs (male and female) did much to enhance their popularity. And many items were made to be used either as figurines or planters. As a rule figurines and vases are prized more than planters. However, Copley seems to be an exception in this respect. The bulk of planters are so beautifully designed they give the appearance of being figurines or artful objects. It is hard to find planters, wall pockets, and vases in good condition if they have been exposed to wet soil and stagnant water for long periods of time.

Copley's vast selection of birds did more than anything else in bringing the name of Royal Copley to the average household. The popularity of Copley really began with the vast selection of birds although a small series of decal bud vases and pitchers was the first to find favor with the general public.

Copley is subject to some crazing with some items crazing more than others. Extremes in temperature, stagnant water, wet soil, and prolonged use of water over a period of time leads to more drastic crazing and spider-webbing. Many lovely items have been ruined through negligent use. Items heavily crazed and stained may be cleared up to a degree by bleaching.

As we mentioned a bit earlier the first items produced by the Spaulding China Company were a series of small pitchers and bud vases with decals of pink and blue flowers on a cream background. These items were stamped "Royal Copley" in gold letters on the bottom. However, some of these very same items can be found with a Spaulding stamp with gold lettering. However, it is safe to say that 95% of the early decal items were stamped Royal Copley and all with a gold stamp.

Royal Copley, the Pride of Spaulding, was produced during the entire time the company was in operation and even during the time of liquidation. Although the Spaulding China Company produced three distinct lines: (a) Royal Copley, (b) Royal Windsor, and (c) Spaulding, it was Royal Copley that constituted about 85% of the entire production.

Royal Copley was sold almost exclusively to the chain stores such as Woolworths, Kresges, Grants, and Murphys. Woolworth was Spaulding's biggest customer for Royal Copley.

Items marked "Royal Windsor" and "Spaulding" were primarily made for jobbers, department stores, and gift shops.

For many the term "air brushing" is not understood. It was the way in which the many colors and combination of colors were applied to the clay figures. Instead of applying the color with a brush in the traditional way the decorators used little spray guns about the size of a pen or pencil with a little container to hold the paint. Each little spray gun was attached to an air supply which enabled the decorator to control the flow of paint through little adjustable nozzles on the end of each gun. Several ladies were assigned to a table with each one performing a specific task in the total operation. Some "dotted" the eyes, some tinted the faces, and others used stencils or masks in creating the desired portions of color here and there. It was a shared operation with each person becoming very adept in her work. As we mentioned elsewhere the decorating department used only women with a certain number being assigned to each table. It was the responsibility of the person in charge of this department to produce a model for each to follow. Just think what 35 women were able to accomplish!

Spaulding produced more birds than any other single item. The bird business mushroomed as we can imagine. Mr. Feinberg estimated that as many as 500 dozen birds (6,000 birds) were made each day. He also estimated that 150,000 dozen (1,800,000 birds) were made each year. Try to imagine the number of birds produced during the entire time of Spaulding!

Without a doubt the company made more money on birds than any other single item. They sold as reasonably as 25 cents at the chain stores with the larger birds bringing more money. The birds selling for 25 cents retail were purchased wholesale at $1.80 per dozen ($.15 each).

Copley's biggest sellers were the following: birds, piggie banks, roosters, the large ducks, and the Oriental Boy and Girl wall pockets. The Oriental Boy and Girl wall pockets were marketed during a time of three or four years when there was a "craze" for Chinese motifs in decorating.

Although Copley was designed specifically for the chain stores, there were times during the war in which some Copley items (particularly the birds) were sold to gift stores and department stores.

How to Identify Royal Copley and Distinguish It From Other Wares

What a challenge identification has become with so many of the products of the Spaulding China Company! Although we are attempting to present the full story of all those items made at Spaulding, our main concern is Royal Copley. Although Spaulding made more than Copley we can safely say that Spaulding was 85% Royal Copley.

What a simple task this book would have been had all items been marked in some way! Fortunately, a lot of Royal Copley was marked either with a gold or green stamp or the name "Royal Copley" spelled out in raised letters. Although paper labels were attached to every item leaving the factory, few have remained for purposes of identification. All in all, there are more unmarked than marked pieces of Royal Copley. However, through study, familiarity, and comparison the following guide lines have become helpful clues in the process of identification.

1. Most Royal Copley is characterized by brilliant color combinations and sparkling designs.
2. If the item appears to be cheap and gaudy one can be reasonably sure it is not Royal Copley.
3. All color and decoration is under the glaze.
4. Never is Royal Copley more than two mold.
5. If an item for its size, is thin and very light in weight, it is most likely an import or the product of some other company.
6. If a bird is heavy, glazed inside and out, and only of one color it is not a genuine piece of Royal Copley.
7. Most of the birds with the exception of the ducks and chickens seem to be associated, in some way, with a tree stump, limb, or knot hole.
8. Most Royal Copley is characterized by detail and novelty of design. We are using the word "most" for a lot of Copley, although pretty, is rather common. There are some very lovely floral patterns, but most of them lack botanical exactness. Therefore, we are forced to use the word "stylized" to prevent any error in identification. The real style, beauty, and detail of Royal Copley can be seen in the many human and animal faces that are found on figurines, planters, and wall pockets. Here, the designers of Royal Copley seemed to "out-

do" themselves. The faces seem to have a personality all of their own and, in addition, they tend to bring out certain realistic human emotions.

9. Although not a hard and fast rule, the presence of parallel runners or ridges on the bottom of many of the items is one of the very important clues in identifying Royal Copley. There are exceptions, but for the most part the presence of ridges strongly suggest that the item is Copley. Great care has to be exercised because similar ridges can be found on many of the Shawnee and Hull items. However, the tendency toward ridges is not wide spread in these lines.

10. As a basic rule the Copley birds do not have **totally** and **specifically** painted-on toes or **totally** and **specifically** painted-on beaks. The beaks, if tinted, are mainly tinted on the upper portion with no specific application of color other than the general blending of body color. We must point out that a few Copley birds appear to have received some bit of hand decorating or brushing at the factory. This is the exception. If a bird has been "touched" at the factory, it is merely that of providing a few brush marks here and there. Please notice it is the non-Copley bird that has specifically and totally painted-on toes and beaks. Most Copley birds are consistently air brushed with no personal treatment or touch of any kind other than that provided by the one who sat at the decorating table.

11. Most Royal Copley items have glazed bottoms because the ridges or runners on the bottom of the items allowed them to go through the kiln firing without getting wiped off. The glaze on the ridges was wiped off as soon as an item was taken out of the glaze tub. The ridges or runners also provided strength for the item. However, many Copley items have unglazed bottoms such as the small banks, so many of the full bodied birds, some of the figurines, and many of the full bodied ducks and chickens. We realize birds are animals, too, but we are doing this for ease of understanding. If a Copley item has an unglazed bottom, it is usually hollow all the way through or has a hole or holes in the center of the base. We have found only one unglazed item that rests flat on the table without any hole or holes in the center of the base.

Royal Copley

Royal Copley Items

Row 1: (a) 3½" x 7" **Floral Arrangment Planter**. Green stamp on bottom. Easy to find.

     (b) 2½" x 6¼" **Sectioned Planter**. Signed with raised letters on the bottom. Made in several sizes and color combinations. Identified as No. 35 on one of the company brochures.

     (c) and (d) are 3½" **Little Ribbed Planters**. The only difference is color. Signed with raised letters on the bottom. Easy to find.

Row 2: (a) 7" **Decal Vase**. Identified as No. 45 on one of the company's color charts. Paper label only. Sometimes this vase is highlighted in blue as well as a deep rose. This is the only Copley item we have that has a perfectly flat unglazed bottom without any "hole" in the base.

     (b) 6¼" **Pink Beauty Vase**. Gold stamp on bottom. Outlined in gold. This is the same vase as shown elsewhere but with a decal of flowers on a cream background. One of the early items. Not easily found.

     (c) 6¼" **Floral Handle Vase**. Gold stamp on bottom. Outlined in gold. More easily found. This is the same vase as shown elsewhere but with a floral decal on a cream background. One of the early items.

Row 3: (a) and (b) are 3¼" x 6" **Coach Planters**. Green stamp on bottom. Item (a) is a kind of beige whereas item (b) is a kind of teal. It can also be found in a deep rose or plum.

     (c) 3" **Big Blossom Planter**. Green stamp on bottom. It is most often found in this color. When found with a green background and yellow blossom it is often called "Daffodil" by collectors. When used with the green Daffodil pitcher it gives the impression of being a part of a set.

Row 1: (a) **7″ Ivy Ftd. Vase.** Paper label only. Easily found. Dark green leaves on ivory background.
  (b) **8″ Ivy Ftd. Vase.** Paper label only. A little harder to find than the 7″ vase.
  (c) **4″ Ivy Ftd. Planter.** Paper label only. Easily found.

Row 2: (a) **6¼″ Ivy Pillow Ftd. Vase.** Paper label only. Pillow vases are more popular and in greater demand.

  (b) **4″ x 7″ Ivy Window Box Planter.** Paper label only.

  (c) **6¼″ Ivy Pillow Ftd. Vase** (Gold Outlined). Paper label only. The gold outlined items are truly lovely and in greater demand.

Row 3: (a) **Handled Leaf Creamer.** Green stamp on base. Made in several colors. It seems strange that a creamer and sugar were made in Royal Copley when no dinner ware was made. Height of 3″.
  (b) and (c) **8″ Daffodil Pitchers.** Green stamp on bottom. The only difference between the pitchers is that of color. If there are other colors we haven't seen them. Very popular and in great demand.
  (d) **Handled Leaf Sugar.** Green stamp on base. Like the matching creamer in (a) it was made in several colors.

Row 1: (a) (b), and (c) are all **8" Floral Beauty Pitchers.** Green stamp or raised letters on the bottom. Rather hard to find. Item (b) seems to be the favorite among collectors.

Row 2: (a) (b), and (c) are all **7" Carol's Corsage Vases.** Green stamp on the bottom. Easy to find. Not pictured is a deep cobalt one which is harder to find. Listed as No. 55 on one of the color charts of the company. This item is named in honor of Carol Phillips of Marshfield, Wisconsin.

Row 3: (a) and (b) are **8" Pome Fruit Pitchers.** Green stamp on the bottom. Rather hard to find. A pome fruit pitcher with a dark green background is found on page 97.

(c) **8" Floral Elegance Vase.** Green stamp on the bottom. A collector of Copley soon realizes that beauty and design are more important than botanical exactness. Rather hard to find. This vase can be found in other colors but the cobalt one seems to be the favorite among collectors. We are naming this lovely vase in honor of Elizabeth and Charles Boyce of Indiana.

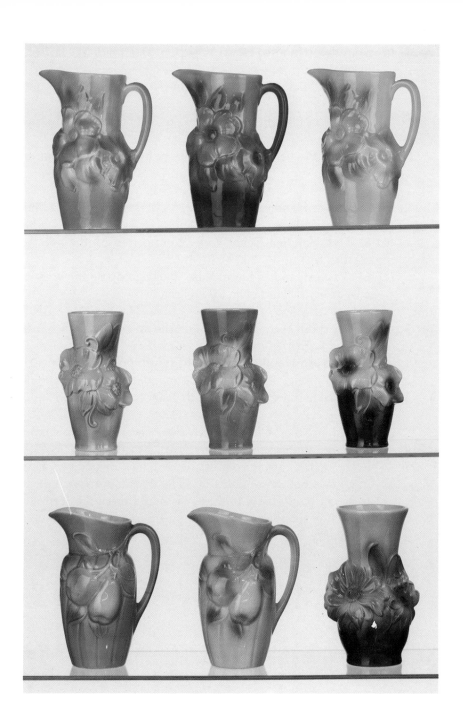

Row 1: (a) 6¼″ **Two-Handled Decal Vase**. Gold stamp on the bottom. Easy to find.
(b) 6″ **Decal Pitcher**. Gold stamp on the bottom. Easy to find.

(c) 6¼″ **Decal Pitcher**. Gold stamp on the bottom. Easy to find.

(d) 6″ **Decal Pitcher**. Gold stamp on the bottom. A little harder to find.

Row 2: (a) 6¼″ **Two-Handled Decal Vase**. Gold stamp on the bottom. Easy to find.
(b) 8″ **Two-Handled Decal Vase**. Gold stamp on the bottom. Harder to find.
(c) 6¼″ **Two-Handled Decal Vase**. Gold stamp on the bottom. Easy to find. Handles are more ornate.

Row 3: (a) 6″ **Decal Pitcher**. Gold stamp on the bottom. A little harder to find with this decal.
(b) 4 1/8″ **Stub Handle Vase**. Gold stamp on the bottom. It is a vase although it has the appearance of being a spoon holder or a sugar bowl without a lid. Easy to find.

(c) and (d) are 8¼″ **Cornucopia Vases**. The gold outline makes this pair more desirable. Item (c) has "Royal Copley" in raised letters on the bottom whereas Item (d) has "Spaulding China" in gold letters on the bottom. The marking on the bottom is the only difference in these vases. Different marks on the same item is not unusual among the many items made at Spaulding. More difficult to find.

Row 1: (a), (b), (c), and (d) are 6¼" **Woodpeckers**. Signed with green stamp or raised letters on the bottom. Designed for use as a planter. Easy to find. Wide variation in color. Item (d) is turned to show the lovely floral design on the stump.

Row 2: (a) and (c) are 5" **Kingfishers**. Paper label only. Rather hard to find. Very colorful. This item was listed as No. 16/1 in the Regal Assortment.

    (b) is a 5" **Blue-bird**. Paper label only. Rather hard to find. Very colorful. This item was listed in the Regal Assortment of the company as No. 16/2. Named in honor of Dorothy Moody of Arcola, Illinois.

Row 3: (a), (b), (c), and (d) are all 5" **Parrots**. This item was designed as a bud vase. Found either with raised letters or a green stamp on the bottom. Yellow seems to be the most abundant color. This item was listed as No. 15/1 on one of the color charts of the company. Abundant. Named in honor of Ron Perrick of Portland, Oregon.

Row 1: (a) and (b) are 7¼" **Cockatoos**. Paper label only. Full bodied. Hard to find. Sought after by collectors. Notice the conspicuous erectile crest. Named in honor of Dr. Lawrence B. Hunt, Ornithologist, Eastern Illinois University at Charleston, Illinois.

Row 2: (a), (b), and (c) are 8" **Parrots**. The parakeets are very similar but have a smaller, more slender body. Note the variation in color. Item (a) is mainly yellow; Item (b) is predominantly blue; and Item (c) is mainly that of a lime green. Paper label only. Full bodied. Prized by collectors. Easier to find than the Cockatoos in Row 1. Named in honor of Mrs. Chris Morrow of Villa Grove, Illinois, who drew the lovely sketches of the paper labels found on the various items made at Spaulding.

Row 3: (a) and (b) are Cockatoos that we are naming **Big Cockatoos**. Height of 8¼". Item (a) has a body that is mainly dark green in color whereas Item (b) has a body color that is primarily pink or deep rose. Raised letters on the bottom. Easy to find. Full bodied. Named in honor of Dr. Iain Paul of Illinois.

Row 1: (a) and (b) are 5" **Larks or Skylarks**. Full bodied. Paper label only. The bird rests on a very fancy stump. We must remember that the Copley birds were not designed for overall accuracy. It appears from time to time, according to our neighbor, Dr. George Godfrey, Assoc. Prof. Scientist at the Illinois Natural History Survey that the artist or designer was endeavoring to capture the overall appearance or Gestalt of certain groups of birds. Therefore the figurines have resemblances of particular orders or families but do not depict actual species. Variation in color. Easy to find.

(c) and (d) are 6½" **Thrushes**. Full bodied. Paper label only. Easy to find. Identified as No. 21 on one of the color charts of the company. Only difference is that of color.

Row 2: (a), (b), (c), and (d) are all 6½" **Thrushes**. Full bodied. Paper label only. Identified as No. 21 on one of the color charts of the company. Only difference is that of color. Easy to find.

Row 3: (a), (b), (c), (d), and (e) are all 6½" **Larks or Skylarks**. Full bodied. Paper label only. Larger than items (a) and (b) in Row 1. Great variation in color. Rather easy to find.

Row 1: (a) **7¼" Swallow on Heavy Double Stump**. Full bodied. Paper label only. The overall design makes this bird a prized item. A bit hard to find. Little variation in color.

   (b) **7" Swallow with Extended Wings**. Full bodied. Paper label only. Identified as No. 35 in the Regal Assortment of Copley birds. Rare. Variation in color.

   (c) **8" Swallow**. Full bodied. Paper label only. This item is the very same bird found in Row 2 below. Not too difficult to find but it is picked up readily by any Copley collector.

Row 2: (a), (b), (c), and (d) are all **8" Swallows**. Full bodied. Paper label only. Great variation in color. Notice that some face to the left and others face to the right.

Row 3: (a), (b), (c), and (d) are all 8" color variations of the **Titmouse**. Related to the chickadee. Notice that item (b) has been given some fancy treatment and it is all under the glaze. We are finding the same bit of decorating on other birds although it was not normally done. Full bodied. Paper label only. A little hard to find. Named in honor of Sharon and Bob Huxford, renowned pottery authors, of Covington, Indiana.

Row 1: (a) 4½" **Nuthatch**. So named from the peculiar way in which it breaks nuts to get the kernel. A little hard to find. Paper label only. Full bodied. Found in various colors.

(b) and (c) are 5" **Doves**. Paper label only. Full bodied. Paper label only. Found in various colors. Rather easily found. Quality of color is a bit inferior.

Row 2: (a), (b), and (c) are all variations in color of what we must refer to as **wren-like birds**. For the sake of reference we are calling these lovely items **Double Birds on Tree Stump**. Paper label only. Full bodied. Rather hard to find. Prized highly. This bird was identified as No. 17 in the Regal Assortment.

Row 3: (a), (b), (c), and (d) are all 6¼" **Tanagers**. Green stamp or raised letters on the bottom of this planter. Notice the lovely color variations. Easy to find. Named in honor of Dr. Richard W. Pippen of Western Michigan University.

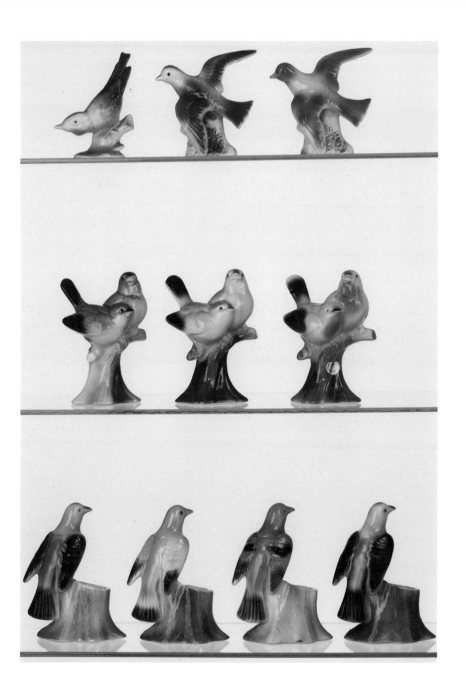

Row 1: (a) 5" **Kinglet**. Paper label only. Easy to find. Aren't the Copley birds lovely? However, identification is extremely difficult as they were not designed to be exact in every way. And we must ignore color a great deal of the time.

(b) and (c) are 5" **Buntings or Seed Eaters**. Paper label only. Hard to find. Notice that items (b) and (c) are a pair which is typical of so many of the Copley items. Again, the character of the tree stump is enough to tell one that it is Copley. Named in honor of Virginia and Lawrence Keefe of Villa Grove, Illinois, who have provided help and assistance all along the way.

(d) 3½" **Little Wren**. Paper label only. Hard to find. One of the smaller birds made by Spaulding.

Row 2: (a) and (b) are 7¾" **Flycatchers or Thrashers**. Paper label only. Hard to find. Extremely fine detail. Named in honor of Mrs. Carol De Moss of Illinois.

(c) and (d) are 5" **Finches**. Paper label only. Hard to find.

Row 3: (a), (b), (c), (d), and (e) are all 6¼" **Wrens**. Paper label only. Easy to find. Notice the wide variation in color. The wrens add a lot of color to any bird collection.

Row 1: (a), (b), (c), (d), and (e) are all 4½" **Vireos**. Paper label only. Easy to find. Notice the wide variation in color. Please remember that accuracy of color wasn't given much consideration. They were designed to be colorful and to sell well.

Row 2: (a), (b), (c), (d), and (e) are all 5" **Sparrows**. Paper label only. Easy to find. Wide variation in color which adds to the beauty of a Copley bird collection. Named in honor of Delores Drown of Ohio.

Row 3: (a), (b), (c), and (d) are all 5" **Warblers**. Green stamp or raised letters on the bottom. Easy to find. Identified as No. 15/2 on one of the color charts of the company. Designed for use as a bud vase. Named in honor of Shirley Graff of Ohio.

The Copley birds, beautiful and lovely as they are, lack exactness as far as color, size, and distinguishing characteristics are concerned. Many were copied from European birds which differ greatly from the American species. Only with the help of an outstanding Ornithologist were we able to come up with a name that would, in some way, help to give these lovely creatures a suitable name.

Row 1: (a) 6½" **Goldfinch on Copley Stump**. Paper label only. Vase or planter. Not too difficult to find.

(b) and (c) are **Gulls** or **Seagulls**. Height of 8" to 7¾". Although they appear so much alike the wings are molded differently. Item (c) has wings that are molded solidly to the body of the bird. The wings of item (b) appear to be applied. Paper label only. Hard to find.

Row 2: (a) 5¼" **Hummingbird on Flower Planter**. Paper label only. Easy to identify. Hard to find. This item was No. 68 in the Lenox Assortment.

(b) 8" **Birdhouse with Bird Planter**. Paper label only. The tail of the bird is smaller than the one shown in the picture. One of the premium items in Copley. Rare.

(c) 5½" **Nuthatch Vase or Planter**. Easy to find. Paper label only. The design of the stump helps to identify this item immediately.

Row 3: (a) 6½" **Big Apple and Finch Planter**. Easy to find. Paper label only.

(b) 7½" **Fancy Finch or Finch-like Bird on Tree Stump Planter**. Paper label only. Rare. Another one of Copley's top of the line items.

(c) 6¼" **Wren on Tree Stump Planter**. Paper label only. Hard to find.

45

Row 1: (a) **7½" Rooster Bank**. Paper label only. Coin slot is at the top of the tail. At the base on the front are the words "Chicken Feed". Base is unglazed with 4 small holes.

(b) The same item as (a) but showing different color combinations. Hard to find.

(c) **7" Rooster Vase**. Paper label only. The high flowing tail adds to the beauty of this vase. Not rare but difficult to find.

Row 2: (a) **8" Rooster Planter**. Paper label only. Difficult to find.

(b) **Hen Planter**. Hen is slightly smaller than the rooster. Paper label only. The hen is as hard to find as the rooster.

(c) **7¼" Common Rooster Planter**. Abundant. Some have a paper label and others are marked with raised letters on the bottom. Height varies as much as one half inch. This planter was listed as No. 64 in the Carlton Assortment.

Row 3: (a) and (b) are **5" Bunting Planters**. Signed with raised letters on the back. Easy to find. This planter was listed as No. 69 in the Lenox Assortment. We are listing this item in honor of Ed Lohr of Villa Grove, Illinois.

(c) and (d) are **5½" Walking Rooster Planters**. Signed with raised letters on the back. Like items (a) and (b) above these planters were made to hang or rest on a table. The white rooster on the extreme right is much harder to find. Few white roosters are found in Royal Copley.

Row 1: (a) 6¾" **Duck and Mail Box Planter**. Paper label only. U.S. Mail appears on the mail box. A rare item.

(b) 8" **Copley Rooster and Wheelbarrow Planter**. Paper label only. Named in honor of Chas. Lumsdon of Illinois. A rare item.

(c) 3¾" **Duck and Wheelbarrow Planter**. Paper label only. This item, like all the action items, is very popular.

Row 2: (a) **Small Copley 5½" Hen No. 1**. Paper label only. The small chickens are harder to find.

(b) **Small Copley 6" Rooster No. 1**. Paper label only. This rooster and its mate above appear to be standing in straw. This is the clue in matching this pair.

(c) **Small Royal Copley 6" Hen No. 2**. Paper label only. The 6¼" mate (rooster) is found on page 97. The clue to matching this different pair of small chickens is the area around the feet. This pair has bases similar to that of the large Copley chickens. Harder to find.

Row 3: (a) 7" **Large Royal Copley Hen**. Paper label only. Notice that the feet do not show in the large chickens. Abundant.

(b) 8" **Large Copley Rooster**. Paper label only. The feet do not show. Color will vary with some of the tail feathers showing either more green or more brown. Rooster is easier to find than the hen. Abundant.

(c) 8" **Large Royal Copley Rooster**. The only difference is that of color. This color is hard to find and prized more by collectors.

49

Row 1: (a) **8″ Mallard Duck on Copley Stump**. This item can be used either as a vase or planter. Paper label only. Not rare but harder to find.

(b) **7¾″ Mallard Duck Planter**. Easily found. Paper label only.

(c) **7″ Mallard Duck Figurine**. Paper label only. The figurine is harder to find than the planter.

Row 2: (a) **Sitting Mallard Planter**. About 5″ in height. Paper label only. Not easily found.

(b), (c), and (d) are the "charmers" of all the Mallards. This is the Smoking Set which is very difficult to find complete. The set consists of 3 ducks with the larger one serving as a cigarette holder and the 2 smaller ones as ash trays. We were fortunate to find the complete set pictured on one of the sheets from the factory. The cigarette holder is 3″ and the ash trays about 2″. Paper label only.

Row 3: (a) **Copley's Big Apple Planter**. Height of 5½″. Abundant. Signed with raised letters on the back of the planter. Made to hang or rest on a table.

(b) **Half-Circle Leaf Planter**. About 4″ in height. Paper label only. The leaves are highlighted with gold. Harder to find.

(c) **Pouter Pigeon Planter**. About 5¾″ in height. Paper label only. Not too difficult to find. Named in honor of Lillian Szafranski of Ohio.

Row 1: (a) 8" "Mill" Plaque Planter. One of the surprises in Copley! It is signed in script in the lower left corner: "The Mill" Amsterdam, Holland, by Jacob van Ruysdael. Made to hang or rest on a table. "Royal Copley" in raised letters on the back. Hard to find.

(b) A similar item without any decal. It is most likely a blank.

(c) 8" Plaque Planter. This one reads "Turner Crossing the Brook" Amsterdam, Holland. Same characteristics as items (a) and (b). Listed in honor of Ed Gisel of New York. Rare.

These Dutch Scene planters were probably designed by Helmuth Sander, who was a Dutch sculptor at Spaulding. Since photographing we have found two more Dutch Scene planters:
(a) "Constable Valley Farm" Amsterdam, Holland.
(b) "Constable, The Cornfield" Amsterdam, Holland.

Row 2: (a) 7½" Deer Open Vase-Planter. One of the five items in the Essex Assortment. This item is the hardest of the open vase-planters to acquire. Paper label only.

(b) 7¼" Bird in Flight Open Vase-Planter. Paper label only. Hard to find. Named in honor of James Ellett of Alabama.

(c) 5¾" Open Fish Vase-Planter. Easy to find. Paper label only. Wide variation in color with other colors shown elsewhere. This item is highlighted in gold which makes it special.

Row 3: (a) 6¾" Fruit Plate Plaque Planter. Signed with raised letters and made either to hang or rest on a table. Included in the Oxford Assortment. Easy to find.

(b) 6¾" Copley Hen Plaque Planter. Signed with raised letters and made to hang or rest on a table.

(c) 6¾" Copley Rooster Plaque Planter. Same description holds as the hen planter above.

52

Row 1: (a) 5½" **Oriental Style Ftd. Fish Vase or Planter**. The two fish appear only on the front side and are mainly blue and pink in color. Paper label only. Easy to find.

 (b) 8" **Cylindrical Fish Vase**. The two fish appear only on the front. Vase is signed with raised letters on the bottom. This vase is beautifully outlined in gold. The fish are green and light brown in color. Easy to find. It was one of the 5 items in the Essex Assortment.

 (c) 5" **Half-Circle Fish Vase or Planter**. Paper label only. Fish are pink and blue. More difficult to find.

Row 2: (a) and (b) are both 5¼" **Open Fish Vase-Planters**. Paper label only. The only difference is color. This vase was listed as No. 660 in the Essex Assortment. Easy to find.

Row 3: (a) and (c) are 5½" **Oriental Style Ftd. Dragon Vases**. Paper label only. The only difference is that of color. Rather easy to find.

 (b) 7" **Cylindrical Fish Vase**. Color and design are very similar to item (c) in Row 1. This same pattern can be found on a 3¾" oval planter. Harder to find.

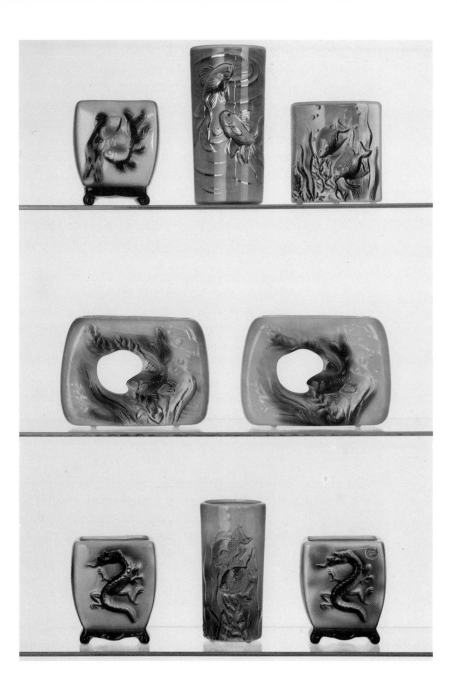

Row 1: (a) 7½" **Wide Brim Hat Girl Planter or Pocket.** Signed with raised letters on the back. Made to hang or rest on a table. The big hat is chartreuse in color which is more difficult to find. Lips are puckered. Girl has right hand under right cheek.

(b) 7½" **Wide Brim Hat Boy Planter or Pocket.** This is the mate to item (a) above. Lips are puckered. Boy has left hand under left cheek. So similar to the girl planter above.

Row 2: (a) and (b) are identical to the Wide Brim Hat Girl and Boy in Row 1. The only difference is in color. This pair is more likely to be found with blue hats.

(c) 7½" **Chinese Boy with Big Hat Planter or Pocket.** Produced in very large quantities. Made to hang or rest on a table. Signed with raised letters on the back. Notice the boy has puckered lips whereas the girls below have smiling lips. This item is shown because a blue hat is harder to find.

Row 3: (a) and (b) are 7½" **Chinese Girl and Boy With Big Hat Planters or Pockets.** The hats are a light gray. This is the color in which this pair is usually found. Again, notice the girl is smiling and the boy has his lips puckered.

(c) and (d) are the very same planters as (a) and (b) above but the hats are yellow and the body clothing is dark green. Like all these planters they are signed with raised letters on the back and made to hang or rest on a table.

Row 1: (a) and (b) are a pair of **8″ Oriental Boy and Girl Planters with Large Basket on Back**. Rare. Paper label only.

(c) **7″ Girl and Wheelbarrow Planter**. Paper label only. Dress is a light green, hat is red, and wheelbarrow is dark green. Not rare but it takes some searching to find it. Named in honor of Betty Bell of Mississippi.

Row 2: (a) and (b) are a matching pair of 4¾″ **Oriental Children with Big Vase Planters**. Paper label only. Included in the Lenox Assortment. Item (a) is sitting with clutched hands beside a teal colored urn or vase and item (b) is happily clutching a teal colored urn or vase with both hands and legs. Easy to find. The company identified item (a) as No. 71 and item (b) as No. 72.

(c) The same item as item (a) above but in a different color. Notice the "writing" on the face of the vase or urn.

Row 3: (a) and (b) are a matching pair of 7¾″ **Oriental Girl and Boy Planters with Basket on Ground**. Item (a) is commonly referred to as the "**pregnant lady**" and item (b) as the "**lantern boy**". Signed with raised letters on the bottom. Easy to find.

(c) and (d) are the same planters but showing a change in color. Here the trousers are chartreuse and the upper part of the garment a dark green. The green color isn't showing up very well. On one of the color charts of the company the "pregnant lady" is identified as No. 15/1 and the "lantern boy" as No. 51/2.

Row 1: (a), (b), (c), (d), (e), and (f) are all **7½" Oriental Boy and Girl Figurines**. Paper label only. We are showing the three colors in which they are usually found. On one of the company color charts the boy is identified as No. 42 and the girl as No. 41. One color is about as abundant as the other. The girl is harder to find. The center pair is yellow and green although the green doesn't show up very well. Figurines are harder to find.

Row 2: (a) and (b) are a pair of **6½" Farm Boy and Girl Planters**. Signed with raised letters on the back. Notice that the boy has a fishing pole but the expression on his face seems to indicate that something else is a little more fascinting. This pair is shown in **green** and **rose**. So that we dare not be sexist let us say that the little girl may be encouraging a little time together. This is one of the delightful characteristics of Copley--capturing ideas, moods, and feelings. Very easy to find.

    (c) and (d) are the same pair with the same characteristics but the color of the clothing is **blue** and **yellow**.

Row 3: (a) and (b) are a pair of **7½" Barefooted Boy and Girl Planters**. Paper label only. This pair is sometimes referred to as the medium-sized hat planters. This pair of planters was included in the Carlton Assortment with the boy being identified as No. 82 and the girl as No. 81. Notice that the girl is smiling and the boy has his lips all puckered for some reason. Harder to find than the Farm Boy and Girl planters.

    (c) and (d) are the same pair with the same characteristics but the color of the clothing is reversed.

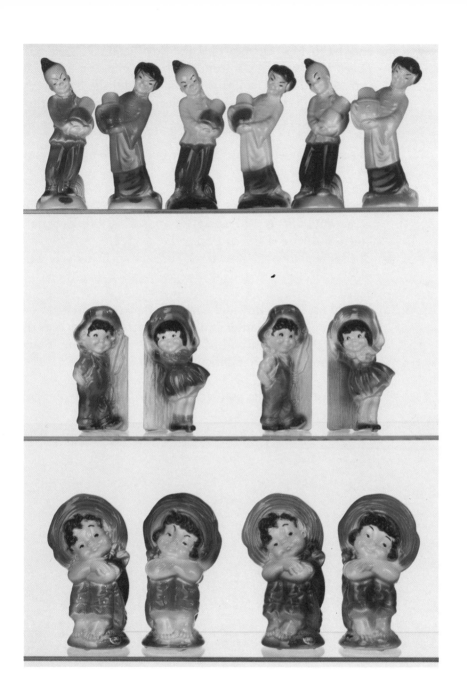

Row 1: (a) and (b) are 5½" **Oriental Girl and Boy Planters**. Signed with raised letters on the bottom. Each is leaning on a vase or urn. Abundant. The girl is on the left and the boy on the right. Colors are a rich rose and blue. Included in the Carlton Assortment with the girl listed as No. 61 and the boy as No. 62.

      (c) The same planter as item (b) above but in a green and yellow.

Row 2: (a) and (b) are **Girl and Boy Leaning on Barrel Planters**. Paper label only. Girl is 6¼" and the boy is 6". Clothing is dark green and rose. Easy to find.

      (c) The same planter as shown in (a) but shown in a lovely dark blue.

Row 3: (a) and (b) are **Dutch Boy and Girl with Bucket Planters**. Paper label only. Each planter is a little over 6". Included in the Carlton Assortment with the boy bearing the No. 78 and the girl no. 79. Not too difficult to find.

      (c) and (d) are the same planters but shown in a different color.

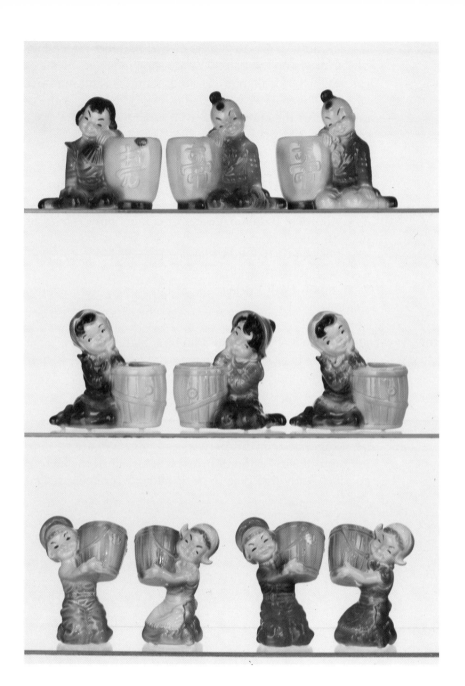

Row 1: (a), (b), (c), and (d) are all **7″ Pigtail Girl Planters**. Signed with raised letters on the back. We are showing some of the colors in which this planter is found. Item (b) is more difficult to find. This planter was listed as No. 53 on one of the color charts of the company. Easier to find. Named in honor of Hildegard Lary of Westville, Illinois.

Row 2: (a) 4½″ **Small Oval Bamboo Vase or Planter**. Paper label only. Easy to find.

(b) 8″ **Cylindrical Bamboo Vase**. Paper label only. This size is hard to find.

(c) 4″ x 7½″ **Oval Bamboo Planter**. Paper label only. Not as easy to find as item (a).

(d) 7″ **Bamboo Wall Pocket**. Paper label only. Rare. Unusual shape.

Row 3: (a) and (b) are **8″ Pirate Head Planters**. Signed with raised letters on the back. Made to hang or rest on a table. Requires a little searching to find this item. The gray head covering is a bit harder to find than the pink or red.

(c) 8¼″ **"Tony" Planter**. Paper label only. Many names have been suggested for this very special item. We are naming it in honor of Mr. Anthony Priola who designed the item. We consider Anthony Priola to be Spaulding's foremost designer. Rare.

Row 1: (a) and (b) are 8½" **Blackamoor Figurines**. Paper label only. Rather hard to find. Designed as a pair.

(c) 8½" **Balinese Girl Planter**. Paper label only. Hard to find. If there is a matching boy planter we haven't found it.

Row 2: (a) and (b) are a pair of 8" **Large Angel Planters**. Paper label only. Hard to find. We are naming these items BIG BLUE ANGEL and BIG PINK ANGEL. We are naming the Big Blue Angel in honor of Rick Summerlee and the Big Pink Angel in honor of Daria Killinger of Michigan.

(c) and (d) are a pair of 6¼" **Small Angel Planters**. Paper label only. The little blue angel is easy to find but the little pink angel is hard to find. We are naming the little pink angel in honor of Nancy Peterson of Illinois and the little blue angel in honor of David Peterson of Illinois. All of the angels, big or small, are made to hang or rest on a table.

Row 3: (a) and (b) are a pair of 8" **Blackamoor Planters**. Signed with raised letters on the back. Made to hang or rest on a table. Easy to find. Item (a) seems to be harder to find.

(c) and (d) are a pair of 8" **Colonial Old Man and Old Woman Planters**. Signed with raised letters on the back and made to hang or rest on a table. These items represent some of the finest work done in Royal Copley. The Old Man is being reproduced in Japan but it can be easily spotted.

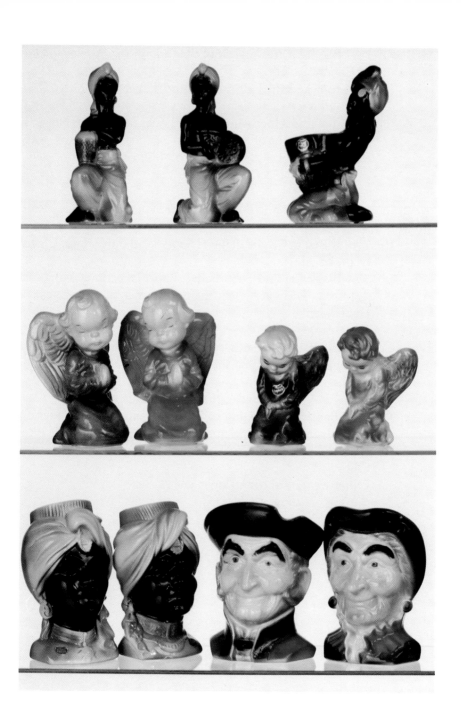

Row 1: (a) 7½" **Playful Kitten and Boot Planter**. Paper label only. Hard to find.
 (b) 8" **Kitten and Bird House Planter**. Paper label only. Rare.

 (c) 8" **Kitten and Moccasin Planter**. Paper label only. Not easily found. The toe of the moccasin is hidden by the cat. Named in honor of Judy Hudson of Illinois.

Row 2: (a) 8" **Kitten in Picnic Basket Planter**. Paper label only. Rare.

 (b) 7½" **Kitten in Cradle Planter**. Paper label only. Rare. Cleverly designed.
 (c) 5¼" **Black Cat and Tub Planter**. Paper label only. More easily found. This cat has all the appearance of a black cat on Halloween.

Row 3: (a) 8" **Teddy Bear Planter**. Paper label only. Hard to find. Notice the open mouth with a sucker in the left hand. All bears are hard to find.
 (b) Same as item (a) but with a more realistic color.
 (c) 8¼" **Bear Cub Clinging to Stump Planter**. Paper label only. More easily found than the Teddy bears. Notice the typical Copley stump. Named in honor of Paul Nowack of Ohio.
 Other bears are found on page 75.

Row 1: (a) 6½" **Kitten and Book Planter**. Paper label only.

(b) 7½" **Cat and Cello Planter**. Paper label only. Hard to find. Named in honor of Dee Long of Illinois.

Row 2: (a) 8" **Black Cat Planter**. Paper label only. So few are found.

(b) 8" **Black Cat Figurine**. Paper label only. Thus far we have found only planters facing the right and the figurines facing the left. Are there mates for each? Harder to find than the planter.

(c) 8" **Black Cat Planter**. The same item as item (a) but there is a good reason why we wanted to show this particular cat. My interest with Copley started with this very item. While in College and struggling to find enough money for Christmas gifts this cat was purchased for my father's gift. Only later did I realize it was Royal Copley. I am showing **this cat** in honor of my late father, Floyd P. Wolfe.

Row 3: (a) and (b) are 8¼" **Kitten With Ball of Yarn Planters**. Paper label only. Found with ease in certain parts of the country. Variation in color. This item was listed as No. 804 in the Oxford Assortment.

(c) 6½" **Kitten With Ball of Yarn Figurine**. Paper label only. Hard to find. One of the members of the Oxford Assortment bearing the No. F25. Named in honor of Laura Erickson of Iowa.

71

Row 1: (a) **5″ Cocker Head Planter.** Signed with raised letters on the back. Easy to find. No. 66 in the Carlton Assortment.

(b) **5½″ Cocker Spaniel with Basket Planter.** Paper label only. Harder to find.

(c) **4¾″ Posing Poodle with Bow Planter.** Paper label only. The poodle is dark in color with a rose bow. Another color is found elsewhere. Harder to find.

Row 2: (a) **7″ Erect White Poodle Planter.** Paper label only. Planter is a shiny black. Hard to find.

(b) **6″ Prancing White Poodle Planter.** Paper label only. Hard to find. In case you aren't a poodle lover, it won't be long!

Row 3: (a) **7″ Pup with Suitcase Planter.** Paper label only. Hard to find. Notice the name tag that reads SKIP.

(b) **7″ Pup in Basket Planter.** Paper label only. Basket is a dark green. Notice the blanket. Sometimes found with a gaudy gold outline which was not done at the factory. Easier to find.

(c) **7¾″ Dog and Mail Box Planter.** Paper label only. Notice the anxious waiting in the eyes and face of the dog. This is a reminder of how we felt at mail time while away at college or during W.W. #2. We are naming this lovely item in honor of the person who first suggested we concentrate and prepare a book on Royal Copley, Mr. Ed Ashley, of Arcola, Illinois. Surprisingly, it is rather easy to find.

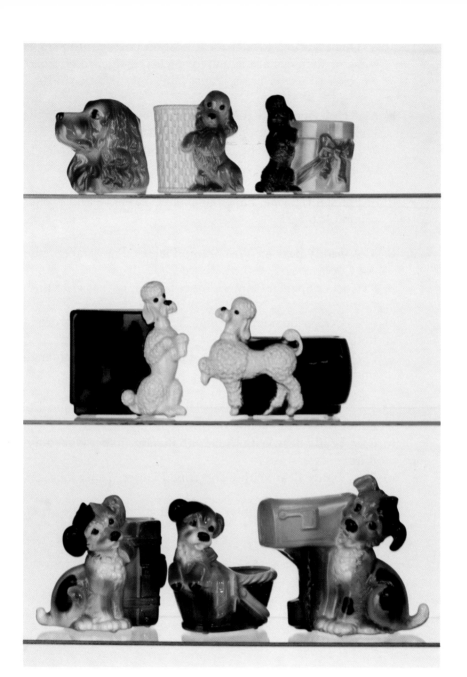

Row 1: (a) **8″ Dog Figurine.** Proper identification poses a problem as some of the dogs are definitely cocker spaniels and others a cocker or terrier cross. Paper label only. Harder to find.

(b) **6½″ Dog Figurine.** Paper label only. One of the items in the Oxford Assortment. Harder to find.

(c) **7½″ Dog Planter.** The raised right foot makes this a more desirable item. Paper label only. Hard to find.

(d) **6″ Spaniel Figurine.** Paper label only. Easier to find. Collar around the neck.

Row 2: (a) **5½″ Teddy Bear on Tree Stump Planter.** Paper label only. All Copley bears are hard to find.

(b) **8″ Cocker Spaniel Planter.** Paper label only. Easier to find.

(c) **6¼″ Cocker Spaniel Figurine.** Paper label only. Harder to find.

(d) **7¾″ Cocker Spaniel Planter.** Paper label only. Harder to find. What a loving face!

Row 3: (a) **7½″ Teddy Bear Bank.** Paper label only. Rare. Named in honor of Warren White of Iowa.

(b) **6¾″ Teddy Bear With Mandolin Planter.** Paper label only. Rare.

(c) **7½″ Teddy Bear With Concertina Planter.** Paper label only. Rare.

(d) **6¼″ Teddy Bear Planter.** Paper label only. Hard to find.

75

Row 1: (a) 8½" **Mare and Foal Vase**. One of the items found in the Oxford Assortment with a suggested value of $2.29 in 1952.
Signed with raised letters on the bottom. This vase seems
to capture the hearts of everyone who sees it. The loving
relationship between mare and foal is readily communicated.
Difficult to find.

(b) and (c) are 8" **Horse with Mane Vases**. Paper label only. Only
difference is that of color.

Row 2: (a) 7½" **Large Elephant with Ball Planter**. Lovely detail. Paper
label only. More easily found.

(b) 6" **Small Elephant with Ball Planter**. Paper label only. Hard
to find. Not as colorful as the large elephant.

(c) 6½" **Peter Rabbit Planter**. Paper label only. Difficult to find.
Named in honor of Dr. Geo. Godfrey, Villa Grove, Illinois.

Row 3: (a) 6¼" **Horse Head Vase or Planter**. Paper label only. Difficult
to find. Listed as No. 74 in the Lenox Assortment.

(b) 4¾" **Full Figure Grazing Horse Planter**. Paper label only.
Very difficult to find.

(c) 5¼" **Pony Planter**. Signed with raised letters on the back.
Easily found.

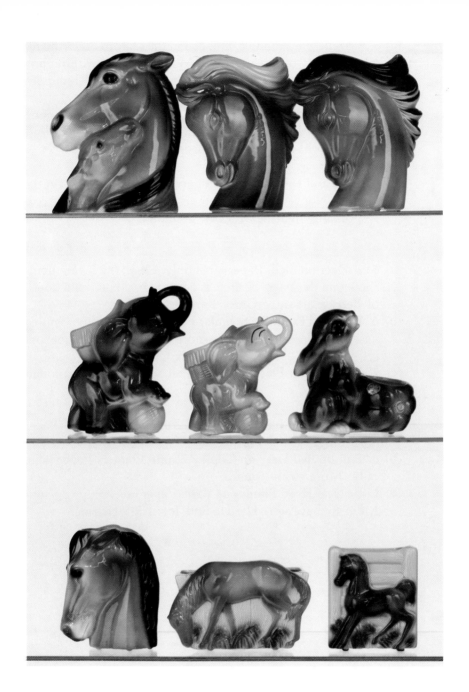

Row 1: (a) **9″ Gazelle Vase Planter**. No. 803 in the Oxford Assortment. Meticulously outlined in gold. Most are found without any gold. Signed with raised letters on the bottom. Abundant.

(b) **8½″ Deer and Fawn Figurine**. Signed with raised letters on the bottom. If only human beings could express such love and warmth! Figurines are harder to find.

(c) **9″ Deer and Fawn Planter**. Signed and raised letters on the bottom. Notice that the planter is always taller than the corresponding figurine. Rather abundant.

Row 2: (a) **6½″ Deer on Sled**. Paper label only. Of all the lovely items shown on this page this item is our favorite. Named in honor of Betty Carson of Ohio. Rare.

(b) **6″ Deer and Fawn Rectangular Planter**. Hard to find. Footed vases and planters are all the more desirable. Paper label only.

(c) **7″ Resting Deer Planter**. Paper label only. Found occasionally.

Row 3: (a) **6½″ Ram Head Planter**. Unusual. Found occasionally. Paper label only.

(b) **8″ Full Bodied Deer on Copley Stump Planter**. Paper label only. More easily found.

(c) **Little Deer Head Planter or Vase**. Paper label only. The only one we have seen. Hard to find. It is a little charmer.

Row 1: (a) and (d) are 7½" **Large Pig Banks**. Paper label and often a green stamp on Item A. Listed as No. 138 on one of the color charts of the company. Hard to find. Various color combinations can be found. Item (d) was made for the Park Natl. Bank of Newark, Ohio. Notice the word "Parky" on the front. Items made for special customers did not have paper labels as a rule.

   (b) 6" **Middle-Size Pig Bank**. Copley paper label but beneath it is a heart-shaped label with the words "**Let me tuck your coins away for what you'll want to buy someday!**" Listed as No. 37 on a company color chart. Color of stripes will vary.

   (c) 4½" **Small Pig Bank**. Color of stripes and basic color will vary. Paper label only. Hard to find.

Row 2: (a) and (b) are 6¼" **Bow Tie Pig Banks**. Paper label only. Hard to find. Variation in color. A later production. The hands can be seen in these pigs whereas the hands are clutched behind the pigs in Row 1.

   (c) 4½" **Small Pig Bank**. This bank has the same kind of labels as the 6" middle-size pig bank. The color of this pig is harder to find.

Row 3: (a) and (b) are 6" **Bare Shoulder Lady Planters**. Listed as No. 73 in the Lenox Assortment. Not difficult to find. Paper label only. The only difference in these planters is the color. Listed in honor of the Camargo Twp. Library in Villa Grove, Illinois. Nancy Jones, Librarian, and Letha Wells and Chas. Knox.

   (c) and (d) are 6" **Gloved Lady Planters**. Listed as No. 67 in the Carlton Assortment. Raised letters on the back of the planter. Harder to find than the Bare Shoulder Lady planter. The only difference in these planters is that of color. Named in honor of Barb White of Iowa.

Row 1: (a) and (b) are 7" **Large Hat Planters**. Made to hang or rest on a table. Signed with raised letters on the back. Cleverly designed. One of the items found in the Oxford Assortment. Easy to find. The only difference between these planters is that of color. Item (a) has a yellow background whereas Item (b) has a rose background.

Row 2: (a), (b), and (c) are 5½" **Small Hat Planters**. Made to hang or rest on a table. Signed with raised letters on the back. Listed as No. 65 in the Carlton Assortment. Easy to find. The only difference in these planters is that of color. Item (a) has a rose background, item (b) has a cobalt blue background, and item (c) has a tan-like background.
each.

Row 3: (a) 6½" x 11½" **Jumping Salmon Planter**. A rare item. Paper label only. There are three rose colored salmon jumping over teal colored waves. Foam is white. A heavy item.

(b) 4" **Small Bowl with Perched Bird**. Found in various colors. Green stamp on the bottom indicates it is one of the earlier items. Very common. Serves many uses.

Row 1: (a) **Affectionate Birds Ash Tray**. Signed with raised letters on the bottom. Length of 5½″. Hard to find. Heart shaped.

(b) **5½″ Leaf and Bird Ash Tray**. Green stamp on bottom. Easy to find. Variation in color of leaf.

(c) **Dancing Girl Copley Lamp**. Original shade. The person or firm making these lamps used Copley figurines mounted on appropriate metal bases. We are showing this lovely lamp to honor Norma Killinger of Michigan. Color of figurine varies. Hard to find.

(d) and (e) are **Lily Pad With Bird Ash Trays**. Green stamp on the bottom. The little bird and lily pad vary in color. About 5″ in diameter. Not as easy to find as the Leaf and Bird ash trays.

Row 2: (a) and (e) are **5″ Leafy Ash Trays**. Green stamp on bottom. Easy to find. Variation in color.

(b) **Oriental Figurine Copley Lamp**. Thus far we have seen only the boy made into a lamp. The figurine was No. 42 on one of the color charts of the company. Hard to find.

(c) **5″ Bow and Ribbon Ash Tray**. Signed with raised letters on the bottom. This tray is found in various colors with various statements in the center of the tray. This one is blue and reads **"Watch those ashes Friend"** whereas another blue one reads **"Old friends wear well"**. Hard to find.

(d) **Colonial Gentleman Figurine Lamp**. Without a doubt this is Copley although we haven't found one with a label. There is a matching lady. The shade is original.

Row 1: (a) and (d) are 7½" **Harmony Vases**. Color is the only difference in these vases. Paper label only. Abundant. Included in the Crown Assortment.

(b) 6½" **Harmony Large Planter**. Paper label only. Easy to find. Included in the Crown Assortment.

(c) 4½" **Harmony Small Planter**. Paper label only. Included in the Crown Assortment. Abundant.

Row 2: (a) 8¼" **Oval Homma Vase**. Black background with white raised stem and leaves. Also found with a dark green background. Named in honor of Tom Homma of Villa Grove, Ill. Easy to find.

(b) 4" **Round Triple Leaf Planter**. Paper label only. The white leaves are found on either a black or dark green background. Easy to find.

(c) 8¼" **Stylized Leaf Vase**. Paper label only. We are using the term "stylized" as many of these items were not designed to be botanically correct. Dr. Richard W. Pippen of Western Michigan University made the suggestion we use the term "stylized" to avoid any serious problem in identification. Easy to find.

(d) 5½" **Stylized Leaf Vase**. Paper label only. Easy to find. Similar to item (c) above.

Row 3: (a) and (b) are 6½" **Footed Bow and Ribbon Vases**. Paper label only. The only difference is color. Easy to find.

(b) 7½" **Philodendron Footed Vase**. Paper label only. Harder to find.

(c) 4¼" **Footed Philodendron Planter**. Paper label only. Harder to find. Since photographing we have found a 4" x 7¼" oval planter which appears to be a center planter for the 4¼" footed planter. It makes a nice set.

Row 1: (a) 8½" **Trailing Leaf and Vine Vase**. Paper label only. Not easily found.

(b) and (c) are **Black Floral Leaf and Stem** items. Item (b) is a planter and item (c) is an 8" vase. Paper label only. Easier to find.

Row 2: (a) and (b) are 7¼" **Hardy Stem and Leaf Vases**. Item (a) has a dark green background and item (b) a black background. Easy to find.

(c) 4½" **Double Spray Planter**. Oval shape but pinched in at the top. Paper label only. Harder to find.

Row 3: All items in Row 3 are **Pink Dogwood** items. All have paper labels.

(a) 8¼" **Dogwood Vase**. This is one of the floral patterns that is realistic. Prized highly.

(b) 4½" **Dogwood Plaque Planter**. This planter was made for the florist trade. This item shows the Lord's Prayer but others can be found bearing various sayings and quotations.

(c) 3½" **Dogwood Oval Planter**.

(d) 4½" **Small Oval Dogwood Planter**. Beautifully designed.

89

Row 1: (a) 9¼″ **Erect Head Mallard Duck**. We are naming it this way in order to distinguish if from the mallard on the right. The female is supposed to be less colorful with the ring around the neck almost inconspicuous. Paper label only. Not difficult to find. Strictly a figurine.

(b) 8¾″ **Bending Head Mallard Duck**. Paper label only. Not difficult to find. Regardless of color and other characteristics refer to items (a) and (b) as an adult pair. Strictly a figurine.

Row 2: (a) 7¼″ **Mature Wood Duck**. Paper label only. Rather hard to find. Designed as a planter.

(b) 5½″ **Wood Duck**. Paper label only. Rather hard to find. Designed as a planter. To avoid further questions we are simply naming this the 5½″ Wood Duck.

(c) 5″ **Duck Eating Grass**. Paper label only. Easy to find. We are naming this little planter in honor of Shirley Charney of Ohio.

Row 3: (a) 6″ **Baby Erect Head Mallard Duck**. Paper label only. A figurine. Not too difficult to find. A set of 2 large mallards with several small ones makes a prized arrangement.

(b) 5″ **Baby Bending Head Mallard Duck**. Paper label only. A figurine.

(c) 5¾″ **Copley Dog Pulling Wagon**. The word "**Flyer**" can be seen on the side of the wagon. Paper label only. Rare. Designed for use as a planter. We are naming it in honor of Betty Newbound of Michigan.

Row 1: (a) 4¾" **Little Riddle Planter**. Paper label only. Shape is more modernistic. Rather hard to find.

(b) 5½" **Salt Box Planter**. Signed with raised letters on the back. Rather hard to find.

(c) 4½" **Dogwood Plaque Planter**. Made for the florist trade. Paper label only. Same planter as shown before (listed with the Dogwood items) but instead of the Lord's Prayer are the words "Count Your Blessings - Hold Each One Dear." Similar planters can be found with other sayings and quotations.

Row 2: (a), (b), and (c) are commonly referred to as **The Dancing Lady**. Height of 8". Seems to resemble Royal Doulton. It was listed as No. 43 on the company's color chart. Item (c) is the color that is hardest to find.

Row 3: (a) 6½" **Indian Boy and Drum Planter**. (We often wonder if an Indian Girl with Drum Planter was made?) Paper label only. Easy to find.

(b) 6" **Elf and Shoe Planter**. Paper label only. Shoe is a dark green. Hard to find.

(c) 6" **Elf and Stump Planter**. Paper label only. Notice that the big stump is what we refer to as the Copley Stump. It was used and carried over on many items. Hard to find. Red hat with dark green clothing.

Row 1: (a) 6″ **Running Horse Planter**. Paper label only. Rather hard to find. Horse appears only on one side. This item can be used also for a vase.

(b) 7½″ **Deer and Doe Planter**. Paper label only. Rather hard to find.

(c) 6″ **Running Gazelles Planter**. Paper label only. Rather hard to find. Notice that all animals shown in Row 1 are in relief.

Row 2: (a) 6¼″ **Water Lily Planter**. Paper label only. Easy to find. Frequently it is decorated in gold.

(b) 7½″ **Fall Arrangement Vase**. Paper label only. Easy to find. Chartreuse background with the plants highlighted in brown. Sometimes this pattern is called **Marine**.

(c) 6″ **Fish Vase**. Paper label only. Hard to find.

Row 3: (a) 6½″ **Kitten on Copley Stump Vase or Planter**. Paper label only. Hard to find. Kitten is gray with green eyes.

(b) 6¾″ **Star and Angel Planter or Vase**. Paper label only. Above the hand of the angel is a depression for a candle. Copley is noted for its lovely angels. It appears to be Copley all the way. Rare.

(c) 8¼″ **Clown Planter**. All evidence tells us this is another unusual Copley item. Hard to find. The unexpected keeps showing up in Copley.

Row 1: (a) **8″ Large Copley Pig Bank**. Made for the sorority whose emblem appears on the shirt of the pig. Below are the words **Fiji Winter Formal** 1959. Red suspenders. Since photographing we have found two more 8″ large Copley banks with the following inscription:
(a) **Midland Buckeye**
(b) **For My Cadillac** - it has a blue bow tie.

(b) **7″ Dog with String Bass Planter**. Paper label only. Very rare. Everything about it is Copley including the tree stump.

(c) **4¾″ Posing Poodle with Bow Planter**. Paper label only. The same poodle is shown elsewhere but in a different color.

Row 2: (a) **3½″ Boat-Shaped Planter**. Paper label only. Turquoise background with brown specks. Designed for the florist trade. A late item.
(b) **10″ Cocker Spaniel Lamp Base**. The unexpected in Copley keeps showing up. A true lamp base. Very rare.

(c) **8″ Pome Fruit Pitcher**. Green stamp on bottom. Yellow fruit on a lovely dark green background. Other colors are shown elsewhere. The Pome Fruit pitchers are harder to find.

Row 3: (a) **5″ Straw Hat with Bow Ash Tray**. Raised letters on the bottom. Gray with a pink ribbon or bow. Rare.

(b) **4½″ Little Imagination Planter**. Paper label only. Black background with design in white.
(c) **6¼″ Small Copley Rooster No. 2**. Paper label only. The matching hen is shown elsewhere. This rooster like its mate has a base similar to that of the large Copley rooster and hen. This variety is harder to find.

Royal Windsor Items

Row 1: (a) and (d) are a pair of **Small Royal Windsor Mallards.** Paper label only. Hard to find. A perfect match to the big pair shown on this page. Some tail feathers are missing.

(b) and (c) are a pair of **Large Royal Windsor Mallards.** In addition to a paper label this pair bears in raised letters the name of the designer, A.D. Priolo. This pair is one of three pairs of Mallards comprising the GAME BIRDS OF AMERICA series. In a company brochure the drake is listed as No. 496 and the hen as No. 495. The drake stands 8½" whereas the hen is 6¼". Hard to find. Color and design is outstanding.

Row 2: (a) and (b) are the **Small Pair of Royal Windsor Chickens.** Large green paper label. The rooster is 7" and the hen a little over 6½". A little hard to find.

(c) and (d) are another pair of **Royal Windsor Chickens.** Crown shaped label of gold and red. These chickens are very ordinary and lacking the quality of the other Royal Windsor ducks and chickens. The rooster is 7" and the hen a little less. A little hard to find.

Row 3: (a), (b), and (c) are all **5" Royal Windsor Planter Plaques.** All are signed Royal Windsor in gold letters on the bottom. Made for the florist trade and referred to as "Books of Remembrance". Item (a) reads "Seasons Greetings", (b) "Happy Birthday", and (c) "Happy Anniversary". Easy to find.

Top Row: **Framed Royal Windsor Mallard Duck**. When we visited Margaret Kadisch, former decorator for Spaulding, she loaned us a brochure that has proven to be very valuable in our research. The company produced 3 pairs of Royal Windsor Mallard Ducks and they were referred to as Game Birds of America. They were a series. The lovely Mallard shown in this picture happens to be No. 496 in the series with its mate having the No. 495. It was drawn and colored by Joan Priolo, wife of Spaulding's foremost designer, Anthony Priolo. Although the Priolos lived in New Jersey they sent sketches to be approved every two weeks. Fortunately this lovely sketch has been loaned to us by the Feinberg family. We are so glad to have an example of what was done before an item was put into production. We have this exact pair of Mallards in our dining room. There is a Royal Windsor green paper label plus, in raised letters, the name A.D. Priolo.

Bottom Row:(a) **10″ Large Royal Windsor Hen**. Paper label only. The large rooster does exist and it is as lovely as the hen. The paper label has a green background with the words "Royal Windsor handcrafted" in gold. We believe this to be the older of the Royal Windsor labels.

(b) **9″ Royal Windsor Madonna Planter**. Signed with raised letters on the bottom. It was identified as No. 351 on a company brochure. A figurine bearing the No. 349 was made also but, like all figurines in Copley or Windsor, it is smaller than the corresponding planter. This lovely and high quality item was designed by Eric Gort, a free lance designer for Spaulding. Hard to find.

(c) **4½″ Royal Windsor Planter**. Signed with raised letters on the bottom. Designed for the florist trade. Ordinary.

Spaulding Items

(All items found on this page have a Spaulding label.)

Row 1: (a) 6¼" **Wren**. Full bodied. This item is really the Copley wren but it is found from time to time with a Spaulding label. Easy to find.

(b) 8" **Jay**. Full bodied. Notice the added "decoration" that adds to the beauty of this bird. Rare. Named in honor of Mrs. Jan Granse, Art Instructor, Villa Grove, Illinois.

(c) 4¾" **Grouse**. Full bodied. Hard to find.

(d) 4" **Small Pheasant**. Full bodied. Hard to find.

Row 2: (a) and (b) are 4½" **Spaulding Pigs**. Decorated in various ways. Designed as a creamer. Easy to find. On the bottom may be found "**Pat. Pending**" or "**Spaulding Pat. 113726**". This item like items (a), (b), (c), and (d) in Row 3 below was personally designed by Irving Miller, Vice President of Spaulding. Application for these patents was made May 23, 1944, with the term of the patent being for 3½ years. This information comes as a result of the courtesy of Rena London, Richardson, Texas.

(c) 4½" **Nuthatch**. Full bodied. Usually found with a Copley label. Found in various colors. A little hard to find.

Row 3: (a) and (b) are 4¾" **Spaulding Chick Creamers**. Easy to find. Decorated in various colors. Found with "**Pat. Pending**" or "**Spaulding Pat. 113724**" on the bottom. We are naming this lovely item in honor of Rena London of Texas.

(c) and (d) are 4½" **Spaulding Duck Creamers**. Easily to find. Found in a variety of colors. Found with "**Pat. Pending**" or "**Spaulding Pat. 113725** on the bottom. Notice the cane under the wing which provides a more novel tail.

Row 1: (a) **Large Spaulding Pheasant**. Included in the Green Stamp (S & H Green Stamps) line during the fifties.

(b) **Spaulding Lamp**. Base is 9″ and the color and decal are almost identical to the Copley vases and little pitchers made at the very beginning in 1942. Most lamps were made specifically for lamp companies and therefore no paper label was applied. This lamp was one of our wedding gifts in 1951 and it may have had a little age before it was given to us. The shade is original although the metal parts and cord have been replaced.

(c) **Spaulding Ash Tray**. Almost 7″ x 7″. U.S.A. is found on the back which is typical of many items made at Spaulding. We prize this ash tray because it was the personal ash tray of Morris Feinberg. He picked it up from a table in his study and gave it to us as a gift.

Row 2: (a) **Large Spaulding Pheasant**. Mate to item (a) in Row 1.

Row 3: (a) **5¼″ Spaulding Boot** (small one). For so long this little boot was the subject of a big controversy for many believed it to be Blue Ridge. Blue Ridge did not make small boots--only a big one about 8″ tall.

(b) **10″ Spaulding Lamp base**. Presence of a Spaulding label on the front near the base. Undoubtedly some Spaulding lamps were sold to department stores. All have the same cream colored background with varying decals.

(c) **6″ Spaulding Boot** (middle sized one). Spaulding made boots in three sizes. Identification is difficult because during this time companies borrowed heavily in various ways from one another.

Solving the Puzzle

For several years a debate has persisted concerning the small boot that many believed to be Blue Ridge (Southern Potteries). Bill and Betty Newbound, authors of *Blue Ridge*, from time to time have indicated in their articles that no conclusive proof existed that Blue Ridge made a small boot. The large boot in Blue Ridge is well documented.

The puzzle was solved on June 7, 1982, when we walked into the Key Biscayne home of Mr. and Mrs. Morris Feinberg. There before us on a table was a small boot with a large one being used as a door stop (filled with pebbles). Immediately, we announced "Blue Ridge--Irwin, Tennessee" only to be told that the two boots were made by Spaulding at Sebring, Ohio. In fact Spaulding made three sizes of boots.

After returning home, we glanced anew at our big break front of Blue Ridge and there beside our big Blue Ridge boot was the small boot we had erroneously been calling Blue Ridge. Although the Newbounds had as much as said so, we had "just hoped" that the pretty little boot might be Blue Ridge.

Now, the puzzle is solved! That little boot is a Spaulding product. The Blue Ridge and Spaulding boots are so similar that identification becomes difficult. Once more we know the reason. During this period of time it was common practice for companies to "copy" and "borrow" from each other. The copyright provisions were such that it was done by most companies.

Some of Spaulding's Special People

Morris Feinberg
President
The Spaulding China Company
1941–1957

Mr. & Mrs. Wolfe dedicated this book to Mr. Feinberg.

This Plaque is one of the cherished mementos that used to hang on the wall of the Spaulding China Company.

Morris Feinberg: 1900 - 1982
"The Heart and Soul of Spaulding"

Morris Feinberg was born January 25, 1900, in Long Island, New York.

He excelled in school, in sports, and in fact everything he attempted. He entered business at twenty with a partner, Irving Miller, importing various household items from Europe. At night he attended New York University gaining a degree in business administration.

On October 31, 1929, Morris married Ida Kuropatkin and in May of 1931 their only child, a son, Joe was born.

In the middle thirties Morris and Irving began to design, assemble, and sell pottery kitchen clocks throughout the United States. They produced the clocks for Sears Roebuck under the "Harmony House" label.

Needing ceramic parts for clocks, Mr. Feinberg made a trip to Sebring, Ohio, a likely center for such needs. While there, the idea of manufacturing art-ware pottery became more than a dream. Early in 1941 the partners bought a defunct plant in Sebring to begin their own production of art-ware pottery. It took unusual courage for a stranger from New York to establish a major plant in Sebring. But it wasn't long until he became highly respected for his business ability and for the simple humanity he practiced as a person.

In 1957, due to adverse trends and changing conditions, Morris retired and decided to sell out. For the next five years he devoted himself to his investments in the stock market and golf.

In 1962 he joined L.M. Rosenthal, an investment banking firm, as the senior advisor. For the next ten years he enjoyed this second act in his business life.

In 1972 he retired from business for the second time and moved permanently to Key Biscayne, Florida.

The last ten years were filled with doing the things he and his lovely wife, Ida, enjoyed so very much. Although this is the story of the life of Morris Feinberg, we must not fail to mention Ida Feinberg, a lady of rare design. Although she remained in the background, she was without a doubt a source of inspiration that gave encouragement to every move and decision that was made.

Throughout the 82 years of his life he gained the love and respect of many people because of his keen intellect, warmth, and sense of humor.

The family as a unit was always his top priority. His perpetual youth and constant optimism were an inspiration to all.

On August 22, 1982 Morris Feinberg died following an accidental fall at his home four days earlier. His last correspondence with me on August 15 ends with these words:

"I am very gratified that posterity is rewarding the creative efforts and high standards that were lavished on Spaulding's production."

After Glow

I'd like the memory of me
    to be a happy one.
I'd like to leave an afterglow
    of smiles when life is done.

I'd like to leave an echo
    whispering softly down the ways,
Of happy times and laughing times
    and bright and sunny days.

I'd like the tears of those who grieve,
    to dry before the sun
Of happy memories that I leave
    When life is done.

Carol Mirkel

James G. Eardley
Spaulding's Man of the Hour

Only rarely does a man like James G. Eardley appear. Here was a man destined from the beginning to be a potter among potters. His grandfather emigrated to the United States from Burslem, England near Stoke-on-Trent, the chief pottery center in England. And his father, Samuel L. Eardley, was the first treasurer of the National Potter's Union when it was organized in the late 1880's or early 1890's in E. Liverpool, Ohio.

James Eardley joined Spaulding China Company when it began operation in 1942 and remained with the company until it was finally liquidated. It would take pages to enumerate all the facets of his busy, worthwhile, and outstanding life. He was a prominent churchman, a highly respected businessman, a man known as Mr. Republican in Mahoning County, a three-time delegate to the Republican National Convention, a 32nd degree Mason, and a veteran of World War I.

His chief contribution to Spaulding was his thorough knowledge of the pottery industry. He was a skilled administrator and organizer without whose leadership the story of Spaulding would have been less prominent. Few administrators were loved and appreciated as much as James G. Eardley. We can say without reservation he was Spaulding's MAN OF THE HOUR.

He passed away on July 3, 1973, at the age of eighty years. His devoted widow, Ruth Hall Eardley, and his daughter, Charlotte H. Eardley, make their home in Berea, Ohio.

"Lives of great men
  all remind us,
We can make our lives
  sublime.
And departing, leave
  behind us
Footprints on the sands
  of time."

—Longfellow

Anthony Priolo - Designer Deluxe

Many factors have contributed to the popularity and desirability of Royal Copley. Without a doubt it was design more than anything else that played the biggest role in bringing Royal Copley to the scene as one of our latest collectibles.

From 1949 to 1955 some of Spaulding's finest work was conceived and designed. This period of time might be referred to as Spaulding's finest hour. Collectors, invariably, in viewing a collection of Royal Copley, are quick to agree that the Priolo items are the most creative and novel of all.

Spaulding items, although beautifully done, were mass produced at a special price for special customers. In no way did these items compare with the fine figurines and art work of the Gort China Company of Metuchen, New Jersey, where Priolo worked before beginning his work at Spaulding.

A brief description of Anthony Priolo's life and work will give us a glimpse of why he was a "designer deluxe" in every sense of the word. After graduating from Westfield High School, he was inducted into the United States Army in 1943 and served in the Pacific. After his discharge in 1946, he went to the American School of Design in New York City where he received his Camouflage Degree (this was his job in the army). In late 1946 he started designing for Gort Bone China producing very expensive figurines. In 1949 he began his work at Spaulding.

When Spaulding shut down, he was invited to work for G. Perlmutter Associates, a firm specializing in the design of furniture and household items.

He and his family moved to California in 1961 where he started his own ceramic business. He stopped doing ceramics when the move was made to Santa Barbara in 1966.

From 1967 to 1981 he specialized in the design of fine jewelry and also taught the sculpture of jewelry at Santa Barbara City College. He is now retired from teaching and commercial jewelry and spending his time with his own sculpture in bronze, wood, and ceramics. He works out of his own shop in Santa Barbara.

His lovely wife, Joan, is no stranger to the field of art and design. One of the very lovely sketches shown in this book is that of a Royal Windsor Mallard Duck. It was from this sketch that the item was approved for mass production. You will notice that the sketch is personally signed by her. We are honored to show a glimpse of her outstanding and creative work.

Truly, Anthony Priolo was Spaulding's foremost designer and deserves the title DESIGNER DELUXE.

"Life gives nothing to men without great labor."

—Horace

Margaret Kadisch
The Lady Whose Fascination With Color Has Touched Us All!

Many persons contributed to the successful operation at Spaulding. We wish we could take the time to mention all names and all people who made significant contributions to the story of Spaulding. Time has taken its toll and therefore we are going to have to give a "blanket thanks" to all those wonderful people who added so much to the "glory" that belonged to Spaulding.

We had the rare privilege of visiting with Miss Kadisch in her home at Sebring, Ohio, in October 1981. Her contribution to Spaulding was recognized and deeply appreciated by all who knew her and worked with her. She was in charge of the Decorating Department at Spaulding from the late forties until 1957. It is obvious from all the lovely items produced that she possessed a rare and gifted talent. In fact she is an artist in her own right. She continues to make her home in Sebring and her gracious ways are matched only by the lovely paintings in her home. We will remember her each time we behold the beauty of Royal Copley.

" A thing of beauty is a joy forever."

—Keats

"An artist lives everywhere."

—Fr.

Pages 119-122 are used with permission of Betty Bell of Verona, Mississippi and Nora Koch, Editor of the *Depression Glass Daze*, Otisville, Michigan.

Page 125: Courtesy of Margaret Kadisch, Sebring, Ohio.

PUPPY AND SPANIEL FIGURINES

6 Inch Puppy and Spaniel Figurines. Beautiful tan coloring with fine glossy finish. 12 pieces each of 2 styles to 2 dozen box.

1E3243 — Per Dozen................$6.75

PLANTER AND VASE ASSORTMENT

Planter and Vase Assortment. To retail from 79c to $1.79. Assortment consists of 15 pieces.

1E3273 — Per Assortment......$10.75

FIGURINE PLANTER AND VASE ASSORTMENT

Figurine Planter and Vase Assortment. To retail from 89c to $2.29. Assortment consists of 24 pieces.

1E3275 — Per Assortment $20.75

The Above Three Assortments Illustrated On Two Previous Pages.

BLACKAMOOR FIGURINES

8 Inch Blackamoor Figurine Assortment. Dark brown bodies with attractive yellow and grey turban and pants. Underglaze colors, high glossy finish. 6 each of 2 styles to 1 dozen box.

1E3247 — Per Dozen $8.50

PLANTER AND VASE ASSORTMENT

Planter and Vase Assortment. To retail from 89c to $2.29. Assortment consists of 18 pieces.

1E3274 — Per Assortment $15.75

HEN AND ROOSTER FIGURINES

Hen and Rooster Ornaments. Newest decorative note for modern and provincial settings. Brilliantly multicolored, highly glazed. Rooster 8 inches, matching Hen 7 inches. Packed 1 dozen assorted Hen and Rooster in carton. Weight 20 pounds.

1E3264 — Per Dozen Pieces..............................$8.50

HEN AND ROOSTER ORNAMENTS

Hen and Rooster Ornaments. Same as 1E3264 except smaller. Hen and Rooster both are 6 inches tall. Weight 22 pounds. 2 dozen assorted in carton.

1E3246 — Per Dozen Pieces..............................$6.00

IVY WINDOW BOX PLANTER

Ivy Window Box Planter. 7 inches wide at top and 4 inches high. Soft cream background with deep green ivy in relief on one side.

High Lustre Glaze Finish.

Self Stand.

Packed 2 Dozen To the Carton.

1E3256 — Per Dozen..................$6.75

IVY BOWL

Porcelain Planter. 4 inches high and 4 inches wide at top with a self base. Ivory color with ivy decoration in relief in natural green underglaze.

Fine Glossy Finish.

Packed 3 Dozen To the Carton.

Weight 3 Dozen, 29 Pounds.

1E3254 — Per Dozen..............$4.25

IVY VASE

Tall Ivy Vase. 8 inches high and 4 inches wide at top. Cream background with dark green ivy in relief on one side. Self stand. Packed 2 dozen to carton.

1E3257 — Per Dozen......................................$7.75

Same as 1E3257, smaller size. 7 inches high and 3 inches wide at top. Packed 3 dozen in carton.

1E3255 — Per Dozen...$4.95

Terms: 2%, 60 Days.

OXFORD ASSORTMENT

Packing: Single Carton Containing 24 Pieces As Follows:

No.	Description	Size	Quantities	Suggested Retail Each	Suggested Retail Total
F24	Dog Figurine	6½ Inches	4 Only	$ .89	$ 3.56
F25	Kitten Figurine	6½ Inches	3 Only	.89	2.67
40	Hat Planter	7 Inches	3 Only	1.19	3.57
41	Teddy Bear Planter	8 Inches	2 Only	1.19	2.38
F42	Duck Figurine	7¼ Inches	2 Only	1.19	2.38
F603	Dog Figurine	8 Inches	2 Only	1.39	2.78
803	Gazelle Vase Planter	9 Inches	2 Only	1.89	3.78
804	Kitten Planter	8¼ Inches	2 Only	1.89	3.78
805	Fruit Plate Planter	6¾ Inches	2 Only	1.89	3.78
901	Mare and Foal Vase	8¼ Inches	2 Only	2.29	4.58
			24 Pieces		$33.26

Weight 36 Pounds Packed

1E3275 — Per Assortment of 24 Pieces — From Stock..$20.75

Illustrated Retail Price Sheet Packed In Every Carton To Aid Retailer In Pricing Items

Terms: 2%, 60 Days.

CROWN ASSORTMENT

Packing: Single Carton Containing 15 Pieces As Follows:

No.	Description	Size	Quantities	Suggested Retail Each	Suggested Retail Total
30	Harmony Small Planter	4½ Inches	6 Only	$ .79	$ 4.74
31	Harmony Vase	7½ Inches	4 Only	1.19	4.76
32	Harmony Window-Box	4½ Inches	3 Only	1.39	4.17
33	Harmony Large Planter	6½ Inches	2 Only	1.79	3.58
			15 Pieces		$17.25

Weight 20 Pounds Packed

1E3273 — Per Assortment of 15 Pieces — From Stock..$10.75

ESSEX ASSORTMENT

Packing: Single Carton Containing 18 Pieces As Follows:

No.	Description	Size	Quantities	Suggested Retail Each	Suggested Retail Total
20	Marine Planter	5½ Inches	6 Only	$ .89	$ 5.34
21	Marine Vase	7 Inches	4 Only	.89	3.56
50	Fish Column Vase	8 Inches	2 Only	1.29	2.58
660	Open Fish Vase-Planter	5½ Inches	3 Only	1.89	5.67
902	Deer Open Vase-Planter	7½ Inches	3 Only	2.29	6.87
			18 Pieces		$24.02

Weight 29 Pounds Packed

1E3274 — Per Assortment of 18 Pieces — From Stock..$15.75

Illustrated Retail Price Sheet Packed In Every Carton To Aid Retailer In Pricing Items

Terms: 2%, 60 Days.

PLANTER OR FLOWER VASE

Porcelain Planter or Flower Vase. 5½ inches high x 4½ inches wide at top. Fish design in relief on one side. Gorgeous blend of maroon, grey and navy blue under fine glossy finish. Self base. 2 dozen in a box.

1E3258 — Per Dozen $6.00

BALINESE GIRL PLANTER

Balinese Girl Planter. Unusually attractive item, richly colored. 8 inches high x 5 inches wide. Dark brown body with grey and green blending into a beautiful combination on turban and pants. Packed 1 dozen to the carton.

1E3248 — Per Dozen $11.50

DUCK PLANTER

Large gracefully designed Duck with open top, brightly multi-colored, fine glossy finish. 8 inches high x 9 inches long. 1 dozen in a carton.

1E3266 — Per Dozen $11.50

PIRATE HEAD PLANTER

Pirate Planter. 8 inches high x 5½ inches wide. Something different. Two-color combinations assorted, red with green and grey with yellow. Natural color face. Packed 1 dozen to the carton.

1E3250 — Per Dozen $13.25

HEN AND ROOSTER

Hen and Rooster Planter. Five brilliant colors, fired underglaze. Rooster 8 inches high. Hen slightly smaller. 1 dozen in carton.

1E3269 — Per Dozen Pieces $13.25

ROOSTER PLANTER

Rooster Planter. 7¼ inches high. 2 dozen in a carton.

1E3267 — Per Dozen $7.75

Terms: 2%, 60 Days.

WATER LILY PLANTER

Porcelain Planter. 6½ inches high x 5½ inches wide. Water lilies in relief on one side. Beautiful chartreuse, white, deep green and blue color combinations with highly glazed finish. 1 dozen in a box.

1E3259 — Per Dozen $10.50

BLACKAMOOR PLANTER

Porcelain Planter or Flower Vase for table or wall. 8 inches high x 5 inches wide. Black face, white and yellow turban. Underglaze colors, high glossy finish. 1 dozen to carton. Weight 1 dozen, 18 pounds.

1E3249 — Per Dozen $11.50

DOUBLE FAWN PLANTER

Double Fawn Planter. 9½ inches high x 5½ inches wide at base. Beautiful high gloss finish over rich two-tone brown. Packed 1 dozen in carton.

1E3251 — Per Dozen $14.95

Royal Copley (DECORATIVE ARTWARE)

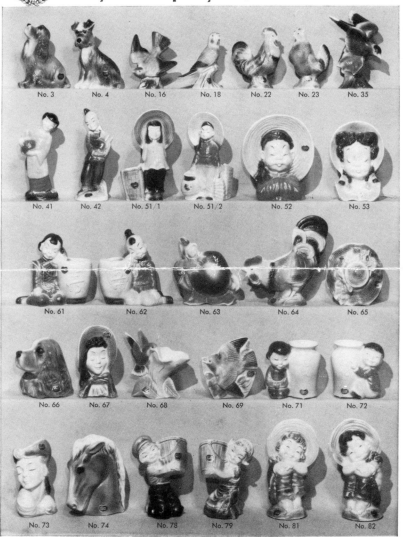

No. 3	No. 4	No. 16	No. 18	No. 22	No. 23	No. 35

No. 41	No. 42	No. 51/1	No. 51/2	No. 52	No. 53

No. 61	No. 62	No. 63	No. 64	No. 65

No. 66	No. 67	No. 68	No. 69	No. 71	No. 72

No. 73	No. 74	No. 78	No. 79	No. 81	No. 82

SPAULDING CHINA CO.   ·   EMPIRE STATE BLDG.   ·   NEW YORK 1. N.Y.

Royal Copley (CARLTON ASSORTMENT)

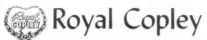

No. 81   No. 82   No. 64   No. 4

No. 3   No. 78   No. 79   No. 65

No. 67   No. 22   No. 23   No. 66

No. 61   No. 62   No. 63

24 Piece Assortment, in Strawless Carton, Packed Weight 28 Lbs.

124

SCULPTORS GALLERY

GAME BIRDS
of
AMERICA

493   494

494   492

495   496

Bibliography and Source Material

Reprints from a 1952 wholesale catalog showing Royal Copley. *Depression Glass Daze*, June 1979. Used with permission of Betty Bell of Verona, Mississippi and Nora Koch, editor of the *Depression Glass Daze*, Otisville, Michigan.

Personal correspondence with Mrs. James G. Eardley and Charlotte H. Eardley, Berea, Ohio, 1981 and 1982.

Original color charts from the Spaulding China Co., courtesy of Morris Feinberg, Key Biscayne, Florida.

Personal interview with Morris Feinberg, June 7, 1982, at his home in Key Biscayne, Florida.

Personal correspondence and phone conversations with Morris Feinberg, 1981 and 1982.

Phone conversations and personal correspondence with Joe Feinberg, son of Morris Feinberg, September and October 1982.

Personal interview with Margaret Kadisch, Sebring, Ohio, October 1981.

An original brochure showing many items made by the Spaulding China Company, courtesy of Margaret Kadisch.

Lois Lehner, "American Dinnerware and Commercial Pottery", *Depression Glass Daze*, September 1979.

Rena London, Richardson, Texas. Copies of Patents on Pig and Duck Figurines designed by Irving Miller in 1945.

Rena London, Richardson, Texas. Photo of Royal Copley, clippings, and personal correspondence, October 1982.

Betty Newbound, Union Lake, Michigan. Article on Royal Copley, *Depression Glass Daze*, August 1982.

Personal correspondence and phone conversations with Anthony Priolo, Santa Barbara, California, 1982.

Sebring, Ohio: A Brief History of Sebring's 50th Anniversary. Library, Sebring, Ohio, 1949.

Price Guide

Page 23:

Row 1: (a) Floral Arrangement Planter ....$8.00-$10.00

(b) Sectioned Planter ....$8.00-$10.00

(c) Little Ribbed Planter ....$6.00-$8.00

Row 2: (a) 7" Decal Vase ....$10.00-$14.00

(b) 6¼" Pink Beauty Vase ....$10.00-$12.00

(c) 6¼" Floral Handle Vase ....$10.00-$12.00

Row 3: (a) Coach Planters ....$12.00-$16.00 ea.

(b) Big Blossom Planter ....$8.00-$10.00

Page 25:

Row 1: (a) 7" Ivy Vase ....$8.00-$10.00

(b) 8" Ivy Vase ....$10.00-$12.00

(c) 4" Ivy Planter ....$5.00-$7.00

Row 2: (a) Ivy Pillow Vase ....$9.00-$11.00

(b) Ivy Window Box Planter ....$7.00-$9.00

(c) Ivy Pillow Vase (gold trim) ....$14.00-$18.00

Row 3: (a) Handled Leaf Creamer ....$10.00-$14.00

(b) Pink Daffodil Pitcher ....$22.00-$26.00

(c) Green Daffodil Pitcher ....$22.00-$26.00

(d) Handled Leaf Sugar ....$10.00-$14.00

Page 27:

Row 1: (a) Pink Floral Beauty Pitcher ....$22.00-$26.00

(b) Blue Floral Beauty Pitcher ....$24.00-$28.00

(c) Yellow Floral Beauty Pitcher ....$22.00-$26.00

Row 2: (a, b, c) 7" Carol's Corsage Vases ....$10.00-$14.00 ea.

Row 3: (a) 8" Blue Pome Fruit Pitcher ....$22.00-$26.00

(b) 8" Tan Pome Fruit Pitcher ....$22.00-$26.00

(c) 8" Blue Floral Elegance Vase ....$18.00-$20.00

Page 29:

Row 1: (a) 6¼" Two-Handled Decal Vase ....$8.00-$10.00

(b) 6" Decal Pitcher ....$8.00-$10.00

(c) 6¼" Decal Pitcher ....$8.00-$10.00

(d) 6" Decal Planter ....$8.00-$10.00

Row 2: (a) 6¼" Two Handled Decal Vase ....$8.00-$10.00

(b) 8" Two-Handled Decal Vase ....$12.00-$16.00

(c) 6¼" Two-Handled Decal Vase ....$8.00-$10.00

Row 3: (a) 6" Decal Planter..$8.00-$10.00
       (b) 4⅛" Stub Handle Vase..$8.00-$10.00
       (c) 8¼" Cornucopia Vases...................................$18.00-$20.00 ea.

Page 31:

Row 1: (a, b, c, d) 6¼" Woodpecker Planters..........................$12.00-$15.00 ea.
Row 2: (a, c) 5" Kingfishers...$18.00-$22.00 ea.
       (b) 5" Blue Bird..$18.00-$22.00
Row 3: (a, b, c, d) 5" Parrot Bud Vases..................................$10.00-$12.00 ea.

Page 33:

Row 1: (a) 7¼" Cockatoo..$22.00-$27.00
       (b) 7¼" Blue Cockatoo.......................................$24.00-$30.00
Row 2: (a, b, c) 8" Parrots...$22.00-$27.00 ea.
Row 3: (a, b) 8¼" Big Cockatoos...$22.00-$27.00 ea.

Page 35:

Row 1: (a, b) 5" Larks or Skylarks...$10.00-$12.00 ea.
       (c, d) 6½" Thrushes..$12.00-$16.00 ea.
Row 2: (a, b, c, d) 6½" Thrushes..$12.00-$16.00 ea.
Row 3: (a, b, c, d) 6½" Larks or Skylarks................................$12.00-$16.00 ea.

Page 37:

Row 1: (a) 7¼" Swallow on Heavy Double Stump................$18.00-$24.00
       (b) 7" Swallow with Extended Wings.........................$28.00-$34.00
       (c) 8" Swallow...$14.00-$20.00
Row 2: (a, b, c, d) 8" Swallow.......................................$14.00-$20.00
Row 3: (a, b, c, d) 8" Titmice...$16.00-$20.00 ea.

Page 39:

Row 1: (a) 4½" Nuthatch...$12.00-$14.00
       (b, c) 5" Doves...$12.00-$15.00 ea.
Row 2: (a, b, c) Double Birds on Stump...............................$24.00-$28.00 ea.
Row 3: (a, b, c, d) 6¼" Tanagers...$12.00-$15.00 ea.

Page 41:

Row 1: (a) 5" Kinglet Planter...$12.00-$14.00
       (b, c) 5" Buntings or Seed Eaters...................................$15.00-$20.00 ea.
       (d) 3½" Little Wren..$14.00-$18.00
Row 2: (a) 7¾" Flycatcher...$22.00-$26.00
       (b) 7¾" Flycatcher...$22.00-$26.00
       (c, d) 5" Finches...$16.00-$20.00 ea.
Row 3: (a, b, c, d) 6¼" Wrens.......................................$12.00-$16.00 ea.

Page 43:

Row 1: (a, b, c, d, e) 4½" Vireos...$10.00-$14.00 ea.

Row 2: (a, b, c, d, e) 5" Sparrows ....$10.00-$14.00 ea.
Row 3: (a, b, c, d) 5" Warblers..$10.00-$14.00 ea.

Page 45:

Row 1: (a) 6½" Goldfinch on Copley Stump ....$16.00-$18.00
   (b, c) Gulls ....$22.00-$28.00 ea.
Row 2: (a) Hummingbird on Flower ....$14.00-$18.00
   (b) Birdhouse with Bird Planter..............................$40.00-$45.00
   (c) 5½" Nuthatch Planter ....$10.00-$14.00
Row 3: (a) Big Apple and Finch Planter ....$12.00-$15.00
   (b) Fancy Finch on Tree Stump Planter ....$35.00-$40.00
   (c) 6¼" Wren on Tree Stump Planter ....$14.00-$18.00

Page 47:

Row 1: (a, b) Rooster Banks ....$32.00-$42.00 ea.
   (c) 7" Rooster Vase...$14.00-$18.00
Row 2: (a, b) 8" Rooster and Hen Planters............................$16.00-$20.00 ea.
   (c) 7¼" Common Rooster Planter ....$12.00-$15.00
Row 3: (a,b) 5" Bunting Planters ....$12.00-$15.00 ea.
   (c) 5½" Walking Rooster Planter ....$12.00-$16.00
   (d) 5½" White Walking Rooster Planter.....................$15.00-$20.00

Page 49:

Row 1: (a) Duck and Mailbox Planter....................................$35.00-$40.00
   (b) Rooster and Wheelbarrow Planter ....$42.00-$48.00
   (c) Duck and Wheelbarrow Planter ....$12.00-$14.00
Row 2: (a, b) Small Copley Hen & Rooster No. 1 ....$12.00-$15.00 ea.
   (c) 6" Small Copley Hen No. 2 ....$16.00-$18.00
Row 3: (a, b) Large Copley Hen and Rooster........................$18.00-$22.00 ea.
   (c) Large White Copley Rooster ....$30.00-$35.00

Page 51:

Row 1: (a) 8" Mallard on Copley Stump................................$22.00-$26.00
   (b) 7¾" Mallard Duck Planter ....$12.00-$14.00
   (c) 7" Mallard Duck Figurine ....$16.00-$18.00
Row 2: (a) 5" Sitting Mallard Planter ....$16.00-$20.00
   (b) Mallard Cigarette Holder ....$8.00-$10.00
   (c, d) Mallard Ash Trays ....$8.00-$10.00 ea.
Row 3: (a) 5½" Big Apple Planter ....$10.00-$12.00
   (b) Half-Circle Leaf Planter (doubtful) ....$10.00-$12.00
   (c) 5¾" Pouter Pigeon Planter ....$12.00-$16.00

Page 53:

Row 1: (a, c) 8" Plaque Holland Planters ....$26.00-$32.00 ea.
   (b) 8" Plaque Planter (Plain) ....$10.00-$15.00

Row 2: (a) 7½" Deer Open Vase-Planter ....\$18.00-\$20.00
       (b) 7¼" Bird in Flight Open Vase-Planter ....\$18.00-\$20.00
       (c) 5¾" Open Fish Vase-Planter (gold) ....\$18.00-\$20.00
Row 3: (a) 6¾" Fruit Plate Plaque Planter ....\$12.00-\$14.00
       (b, c) 6¾" Hen and Rooster Plaque Planters..............\$16.00-\$20.00 ea.

Page 55:
Row 1: (a) 5½" Oriental Style Fish Vase ....\$8.00-\$10.00
       (b) 8" Cylindrical Fish Vase (gold trim).....................\$14.00-\$18.00
       (c) 5" Half-Circle Fish Vase-Planter ....\$14.00-\$16.00
Row 2: (a, b) 5¼" Open Fish Vase-Planters............................\$12.00-\$14.00 ea.
Row 3: (a, c) 5½" Oriental Style Ftd. Dragon Vase-Planters......\$8.00-\$10.00 ea.
       (b) 7" Cylindrical Fish Vase ....\$12.00-\$14.00

Page 57:
Row 1: (a, b) 7½" Wide Brim Girl and Boy Planters...............\$22.00-\$28.00 ea.
Row 2: (a, b) 7½" Wide Brim Boy and Girl Planters...............\$22.00-\$28.00 ea.
       (c) 7½" Chinese Boy Big Hat Planter...........................\$18.00-\$20.00
Row 3: (a, b, c, d) 7½" Chinese Girl and Boy
       with Big Hat Planters ....\$18.00-20.00 ea.

Page 59:
Row 1: (a, b) 8" Oriental Boy and Girl
       with Large Basket on Back..\$22.00-\$28.00 ea.
       (c) 7" Girl and Wheelbarrow.......................................\$14.00-\$18.00
Row 2: (a, b, c) 4¾" Oriental Children
       with Big Vase Planters..\$8.00-\$10.00 ea.
Row 3: (a, b, c, d) 7¾" Oriental Girl and Boy
       Planters with Basket on Ground ....\$12.00-\$14.00 ea.

Page 61:
Row 1: (a, b) 7½" Oriental Boy and Girl Figurines ....\$12.00-\$15.00 ea.
       (c, d) 7½" Oriental Boy and Girl Figurines ....\$12.00-\$15.00 ea.
       (e, f) 7½" Oriental Boy and Girl Figurines ....\$12.00-\$15.00 ea.
Row 2: (a, b, c, d) 6½" Farm Boy and Girl Planters................\$14.00-\$18.00 ea.
Row 3: (a, b, c, d) 7½" Barefooted Boy and Girl Planters.......\$16.00-\$20.00 ea.

Page 63:
Row 1: (a, b, c) 5½" Oriental Girl and Boy Planters...............\$10.00-\$12.00 ea.
Row 2: (a, b, c) Girl and Boy Leaning on Barrel Planters ......\$12.00-\$15.00 ea.
Row 3: (a, b, c, d) Dutch Boy & Girl w/Bucket Planters ....\$12.00-\$15.00 ea.

Page 65:
Row 1 (a, c, d) 7" Pigtail Girl Planters ....\$18.00-\$20.00 ea.
       (b) 7" Pigtail Girl Planter...\$18.00-\$22.00

Row 2: (a) 4½" Small Oval Bamboo Planter..............................$6.00-$8.00
      (b) 8" Bamboo Cylindrical Vase................................$10.00-$12.00
      (c) 4"x 7" Oval Bamboo Planter ....$10.00-$12.00
      (d) 7" Bamboo Wall Pocket...$25.00-$30.00
Row 3: (a, b) 8" Pirate Head Planters.............................$26.00-$32.00 ea.
      (c) 8¼" Tony Planter..$30.00-$38.00

Page 67:

Row 1: (a, b) 8½" Blackamoor Figurines ....$18.00-$20.00 ea.
      (c) 8½" Balinese Girl Planter ....$14.00-$18.00
Row 2: (a, b) 8" Large Blue and Pink Angels.........................$20.00-$25.00 ea.
      (c) 6¼" Small Blue Angel...$14.00-$18.00
      (d) 6¼" Small Pink Angel..$16.00-$22.00
Row 3: (a, b) 8" Blackamoor Planters.................................$24.00-$28.00 ea.
      (c, d) 8" Colonial Old Man and Woman Planters......$25.00-$30.00 ea.

Page 69:

Row 1: (a) 7½" Playful Kitten and Boot Planter ....$25.00-$30.00
      (b) 8" Kitten and Bird House Planter.........................$35.00-$40.00
      (c) 8" Kitten and Moccasin Planter............................$22.00-$26.00
Row 2: (a) 8" Kitten in Picnic Basket Planter ....$45.00-$50.00
      (b) 7½" Kitten in Cradle Planter.................................$32.00-$40.00
      (c) 5¼" Black Cat and Tub Planter ....$14.00-$18.00
Row 3: (a, b) 8" Teddy Bear Planters ....$28.00-$34.00 ea.
      (c) 8¼" Bear Cub Clinging to Stump Planter.............$22.00-$25.00

Page 71:

Row 1: (a) 6½" Kitten and Book Planter ....$16.00-$20.00
      (b) 7½" Cat and Cello Planter....................................$35.00-$40.00
Row 2: (a, c) 8" Black Cat Planters ....$16.00-$20.00 ea.
      (b) 8" Black Cat Figurine...$24.00-$28.00
Row 3: (a) 8¼" Kitten with Red Ball of Yarn Planter.............$24.00-$30.00
      (b) 8¼" Kitten with Yellow Ball of Yarn Planter........$16.00-$20.00
      (c) 6½" Kitten with Ball of Yarn Figurine..................$20.00-$26.00

Page 73:

Row 1: (a) 5" Cocker Head Planter...$8.00-$12.00
      (b) 5½" Cocker Spaniel with Basket Planter..............$12.00-$15.00
      (c) 4¾" Posing Poodle with Bow Planter...................$14.00-$18.00
Row 2: (a) 7" Erect White Poodle Planter ....$16.00-$22.00
      (b) 6" Prancing White Poodle Planter ....$16.00-$22.00
Row 3: (a) 7" Pup with Suitcase Planter $20.00-25.00
      (b) 7" Pup in Basket Planter.......................................$14.00-$18.00
      (c) 7¾" Dog and Mail Box Planter.............................$15.00-$20.00

Page 75:

Row 1: (a) 8" Figurine...$18.00-$22.00
      (b) 6½" Dog Figurine ....$14.00-$18.00
      (c) 7½" Dog Figurine ....$24.00-$30.00
      (d) 6" Spaniel Figurine..$12.00-$15.00

Row 2: (a) 5½" Teddy Bear on Tree Stump Planter ....$15.00-$20.00
      (b) 8" Cocker Spaniel Figurine ....$15.00-$20.00
      (c) 6¼" Cocker Spaniel Figurine ....$15.00-$20.00
      (d) 7¾" Cocker Spaniel Planter ....$14.00-$18.00

Row 3: (a) Teddy Bear Bank...$40.00-$45.00
      (b) Teddy Bear with Mandolin Planter.......................$28.00-$36.00
      (c) Teddy Bear with Concertina Planter.....................$40.00-$48.00
      (d) 6¼" Teddy Bear Planter..$20.00-$25.00

Page 77:

Row 1: (a) 8½" Mare and Foal Vase..$22.00-$27.00
      (b) 8" Horse with Mane Vase ....$16.00-$22.00
      (c) 8" Horse with Mane Vase ....$24.00-$28.00

Row 2: (a) 7½" Large Elephant with Ball Planter ....$20.00-$25.00
      (b) 6" Small Elephant with Ball Planter ....$15.00-$20.00
      (c) 6½" Peter Rabbit Planter ....$24.00-$28.00

Row 3: (a) 6¼" Horse Head Vase...$12.00-$16.00
      (b) 4¾" Full Figure Grazing Horse Planter ....$20.00-$28.00
      (c) 5½" Pony Planter...$10.00-$12.00

Page 79:

Row 1: (a) 9" Gazelle Vase Planter ....$18.00-$24.00
      (b) 8½" Deer and Fawn Figurine...............................$18.00-$24.00
      (c) 9" Deer and Fawn Planter......................................$16.00-$22.00

Row 2: (a) 6½" Deer on Sled ....$20.00-$25.00
      (b) 6" Deer and Fawn Rectangular Planter ....$17.00-$21.00
      (c) 7" Resting Deer Planter ....$15.00-$20.00

Row 3: (a) 6½" Ram Head Planter ....$16.00-$20.00
      (b) 8" Full Bodied Deer on Copley Stump Planter....$16.00-$20.00
      (c) 7⅛" Little Deer Head Planter................................$12.00-$18.00

Page 81:

Row 1: (a, d) 7½" Large Pig Banks ....$26.00-$32.00 ea.
      (b) 6" Middle-Size Pig Bank ....$25.00-$30.00
      (c) 4½" Small Pig Bank..$20.00-$26.00

Row 2: (a, b) 6¼" Bow Tie Pig Banks ....$18.00-$24.00
      (c) 4½" Small Pig Bank..$20.00-$25.00

Row 3: (a, b) 6" Bare Shoulder Lady Planters ....$18.00-$20.00 ea.
      (c, d) 6" Gloved Lady Planters...................................$18.00-$20.00 ea.

Page 83:

Row 1: (a, b) 7" Large Hat Planters...$15.00-$20.00 ea.
Row 2: (a, b, c) 5½" Small Hat Planters ....$15.00-$20.00 ea.
Row 3: (a) 6½" x 11½" Jumping Salmon Planter....................$35.00-$45.00
      (b) 4" Small Bowl with Perched Bird ....$8.00-$10.00

Page 85:

Row 1: (a) 5½" Affectionate Birds Ash Tray ....$12.00-$16.00
      (b) 5½" Leaf and Bird Ash Tray ....$6.00-$9.00
      (c) Dancing Lady or Girl Lamp...................................$40.00-$50.00
      (d, e) 5" Lily Pad with Bird Ash Trays ....$6.00-$9.00 ea.
Row 2: (a, e) 5" Leafy Ash Trays ....$5.00-$6.00 ea.
      (b) Oriental Figurine Copley Lamp ....$25.00-$30.00
      (c) 5" Bow and Ribbon Ash Tray................................$15.00-$20.00
      (d) Colonial Gentleman Figurine Lamp (doubtful) ..$20.00-$25.00

Page 87:

Row 1: (a,d) 7½" Harmony Vases ....$8.00-$12.00 ea.
      (b) 6½" Harmony Large Planter...............................$8.00-$12.00
      (c) 4½" Harmony Small Planter...................................$6.00-$8.00
Row 2: (a) 8¼" Oval Homma Vase ....$8.00-$12.00
      (b) 4" Round Triple Leaf Planter................................$10.00-$14.00
      (c) 8¼" Stylized Leaf Vase ....$8.00-$10.00
      (d) 5½" Stylized Leaf Vase ....$6.00-$8.00
Row 3: (a, b) 6½" Ftd. Bow and Ribbon Vase ....$8.00-$12.00 ea.
      (c) 7½" Philodendron Footed Vase ....$8.00-$12.00
      (d) 4¼" Philodendron Planter......................................$6.00-$8.00

Page 89:

Row 1: (a) 8½" Trailing Leaf and Vine Vase ....$10.00-$15.00
      (b) 4⅛" Small Black Floral Leaf and Stem Planter.........$6.00-$9.00
      (c) 8" Black Floral Leaf and Stem Vase.........................$8.00-$12.00
Row 2: (a, b) 7¼" Hardy Stem and Leaf Vase....................$10.00-$15.00 ea.
      (c) 4¼" Double Spray Planter....................................$8.00-$10.00
Row 3: (a) 8¼" Dogwood Vase..$15.00-$18.00
      (b) 4½" Dogwood Plaque Planter ....$12.00-$15.00
      (c) 3½" Dogwood Oval Planter...................................$8.00-$12.00
      (d) 4½" Small Oval Dogwood Planter.........................$8.00-$10.00

Page 91:

Row 1: (a, b) Large 9¼" Erect Head and 8¾" Large
      Bending Head Mallards ....$20.00-$25.00 ea.
Row 2: (a) 7¼" Mature Wood Duck Planter..........................$14.00-$18.00
      (b) 5½" Wood Duck Planter.......................................$10.00-$15.00
      (c) 5" Duck Eating Grass Planter.................................$8.00-$12.00

Row 3: (a, b) Small Erect and Bending Head Mallards ....$10.00-$15.00 ea.
       (c) 5¾" Copley Dog Pulling Wagon...........................$16.00-$22.00

Page 93:

Row 1: (a) 4¾" Little Riddle Planter..$10.00-$12.00
       (b) 5½" Salt Box Planter...$16.00-$20.00
       (c) 4½" Dogwood Plaque Planter ....$12.00-$15.00
Row 2: (a, b) 8" Dancing Lady Figurines ....$32.00-$38.00
       (c) 8" Dancing Lady Figurine.....................................$36.00-$40.00
Row 3: (a) 6½" Indian Boy and Drum Planter ....$10.00-$15.00
       (b) 6" Elf and Shoe Planter..$15.00-$20.00
       (c) 6" Elf and Stump Planter..$15.00-$20.00

Page 95:

Row 1: (a) 6" Running Horse Planter..$9.00-$12.00
       (b) 7½" Deer and Doe or Antelope Planter ....$9.00-$12.00
       (c) 6" Running Gazelles Planter....................................$9.00-$12.00
Row 2: (a) Water Lily Planter..$8.00-$10.00
       (b) 7½" Fall Arrangement Planter................................$9.00-$12.00
       (c) 6" Fish Vase (figurine) ....$25.00-$30.00
Row 3: (a) 6½" Kitten on Copley Stump Planter ....$18.00-$22.00
       (b) 6¾" Star and Angel Planter....................................$18.00-$22.00
       (c) 8¼" Clown Planter ....$28.00-$32.00

Page 97:

Row 1: (a) 8" Large Pig Bank..$26.00-$32.00
       (b) 7" Dog with String Bass Planter ....$45.00-$50.00
       (c) 4¾" Posing Poodle with Bow Planter...................$14.00-$18.00
Row 2: (a) 3½" Boat-Shaped Planter..$8.00-$10.00
       (b) 10" Cocker Spaniel Lamp Base................................$36.00-$46.00
       (c) 8" Pome Fruit Pitcher ....$22.00-$26.00
Row 3: (a) 5" Straw Hat with Bow Ash Tray ....$10.00-$12.00
       (b) 4½" Little Imagination Planter ....$8.00-$10.00
       (c) 6¼" Small Copley Rooster No. 2 ....$16.00-$18.00

Page 99:

Row 1: (a, d) Small Royal Windsor Unsigned
       Priolo Mallards..$28.00-$34.00 ea.
       (b, c) Priolo Signed Royal Windsor Mallards ....$50.00-$60.00 ea.
Row 2: (a, b) 7" and 6½" Small Royal Windsor Chickens......$16.00-$18.00 ea.
       (c, d) 7" and 6½" Royal Windsor Chickens.................$12.00-$16.00 ea.
Row 3: (a, b, c) Royal Windsor Planter Plaques.......................$8.00-$10.00

Page 101:

Row 1: (a) Original Priolo Drawing of Mallards....................................NPA

Row 2: (a) 10" Large Royal Windsor Hen ....$40.00-$45.00
      (b) 9" Royal Windsor Madonna Planter ....$22.00-$26.00
      (c) 4½" Royal Windsor Planter ....$8.00-$10.00

Page 103:

Row 1: (a) 6¼" Wren ....$12.00-$16.00
      (b) 8" Spaulding Jay ....$22.00-$30.00
      (c) 4¾" Grouse ....$15.00-$20.00
      (d) 4" Small Pheasant ....$14.00-$16.00
Row 2: (a, b) 4½" Spaulding Pig Creamers ....$10.00-$15.00 ea.
      (c) 4½" Nuthatch ....$12.00-$14.00
Row 3: (a, b) 4¾" Spaulding Chick Creamers ....$10.00-$15.00 ea.
      (c, d) 4½" Spaulding Duck Creamers ....$10.00-$15.00 ea.

Page 105:

Row 1: (a) Large Spaulding Pheasant ....$15.00-$20.00
      (b) 9" Spaulding Lamp Base ....$25.00-$30.00
      (c) 7" x 7" Spaulding Ash Tray ....$10.00-$15.00
Row 2: (a) Large Spaulding Pheasant ....$15.00-$20.00
Row 3: (a) 5¼" Spaulding Boot ....$12.00-$16.00
      (b) 10" Spaulding Lamp Base ....$30.00-$35.00
      (c) 6" Spaulding Boot ....$12.00-$16.00

NPA–No Price Available

Schroeder's Antiques Price Guide

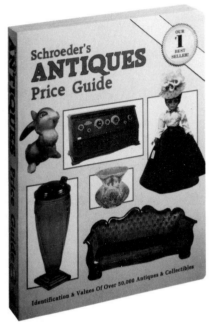

Schroeder's Antiques Price Guide has become THE household name in the antiques and collectibles field. Our team of editors work year around with more than 200 contributors to bring you our #1 best-selling book on antiques and collectibles.

With more than 50,000 items identified and priced, *Schroeder's* is a must for the collector and dealer alike. If it merits the interest of today's collector, you'll find it in *Schroeder's*. Each subject is represented with histories and background information. In addition, hundreds of sharp original photos are used each year to illustrate not only the rare and unusual, but the everyday "fun-type" collectibles as well – not postage stamp pictures, but large close-up shots that show important details clearly.

Our editors compile a new book each year. Never do we merely change prices. Each category is thoroughly checked to spot inconsistencies, listings that may not be entirely reflective of actual market dealings, and lines too vague to be of merit. Only the best of the lot remains for publication. You'll find *Schroeder's Antiques Price Guide* the one to buy for factual information and quality.

8½x11", 608 Pages   **$12.95**

COLLECTOR BOOKS

A Division of Schroeder Publishing Co., Inc.